MORE
UNSUNG
HER**O**ES

(and a Few *More* Villains)

WANDA ROBINSON

GOSPEL
ADVOCATE
A TRUSTED NAME SINCE 1855

Published by Gospel Advocate Co.
1006 Elm Hill Pike, Nashville, TN 37210
www.gospeladvocate.com

ISBN: 978-0-89225-667-9

Dedication

Dedicated to my three children, Christopher, Stephanie and Warren, who have enriched my life with love and joy as I have watched them grow into faithful Christian adults now guiding their own children in the ways of the Lord.

Table of CONTENTS

Introduction

Bible puzzles and tests assess our knowledge of the Scriptures. I especially enjoy taking Bible quizzes with multiple choice answers. I do pretty well on the easy questions and even the moderate ones, but the difficult ones, not so much. On the extreme ones I rarely get any right. See how well you do on this little test. The answers are at the end, but don't peek!

EASY

1. Who asked Jesus to perform His first recorded miracle?

    A. Peter

    B. Martha

    C. Pilate

    D. Mary, His mother

MODERATE

2. Who deserted Paul and Barnabas at Pamphylia?

    A. Timothy

    B. Silas

    C. Simon Peter

    D. John Mark

DIFFICULT

3. Who said, "Thus says the Holy Spirit, 'So shall the Jews at Jerusalem bind the man who owns this belt, and deliver him into the hands of the Gentiles'"?

    A. Sergius Paulus

    B. Caiaphas

C. Agabus

D. Apollos

EXTREME

4. Who was Nicolas?

A. A eunuch of Ethiopia

B. A proselyte of Antioch

C. A Jew from the area of Antioch who hindered Paul

D. A Pharisee who advised the high priest in Jerusalem

E. A wealthy man of the city of Laodicea

5. What was the name of the steward who was married to Joanna?

A. Claudia

B. Cleopas

C. Crescens

D. Chuza

E. Clement

6. Which of these people were not among the names listed in the closing chapter of Romans?

A. Sosipater

B. Quartus

C. Phygelus

D. Epaenetus

E. Andronicus

How did you do? Don't worry if you missed one or even several. Most of these Bible characters are mentioned only briefly, but they're important nonetheless. They provide us examples of how to live our lives and direction for how to live for God. In this study, we will look at several men in the New Testament who may or may not be familiar to you, men like Thomas, Demas, Eutychus, Barnabas, and Onesimus.

These unsung heroes (and a few villains) of the Bible were real people with real thoughts, emotions, desires and fears, just as we have. We do not need to see them as people far removed from us by time, circumstances or character, for they were humans created by the same almighty God who created us. They worked; they had families; they loved; they laughed; they cried. Some believed in Jesus as the Son of God; some had doubts. Some lived faithfully all of their lives; others were drawn away by Satan. When we struggle as these men did, we can be strengthened by remembering how they handled their struggles. When we are fearful, we can gain courage by thinking about how they overcame scary situations. When we have bad attitudes, we can bear in mind the strategies they used to rise above their harmful thoughts. Sometimes they will have set positive examples for us to follow; other times we will find negative examples to avoid.

Following the examples of others is in itself a very biblical principle. Jehoshaphat had examples to follow, both good and bad, but he chose to follow the good example set by his ancestor David (2 Chronicles 17:3-4). He could just as easily have followed in the same path as the rest of Israel, worshiping false idols, but his decision was to model his life in such a way as to be obedient to God. As we consider these lesser-known men of the New Testament, both the heroes and the villains, let us strive to learn from them how best to please God.

Answers
1. D – John 2:3; 2. D – Acts 13:13; 3. C – Acts 21:10-11; 4. B – Acts 6:1-6; 5. D – Luke 8:3; 6. C – Romans 16

ZACCHAEUS:

Little Man, Big Heart

Luke 19:1-10

I'm so excited because I'm going to be rich! Just look at this email I recently received:

Dear Friend,

My name is Col. Brian Dennison Kent, a U.S. Army officer serving in the 3rd Infantry Division in Iraq. I want you to read this mail carefully and understand it. In 2003, my men and I found over $900 million in Saddam Hussein's hideout in Baghdad. We sent some back to the Iraq government after counting it in a classified location, but we also kept some behind for ourselves. Some of the money we shared among ourselves was worth over $200 million.

I need someone to help me; I found a secured way of getting the package out of Iraq for you to pick up through the help of a U.N. humanitarian officer on peacekeeping. I just need someone I can trust. The total amount of money is $10 million.

If you can handle this deal let me know immediately; you will receive 20 percent of the money. All you need to do is find a safe place where you can keep the box till I leave Iraq. Regards,

Col. Brian D. Kent,
U.S. Military, Baghdad, Iraq

What? You don't think I'm going to be rich? But money is so important and being rich would give me the opportunity to help others and enjoy myself and do all kinds of things.

Well, you're right. This email is a scam, and it's not going to make me rich. However, one particular man we read about in the Scriptures had plenty of money. Thankfully, he discovered riches are not always what they are cracked up to be. This is a man familiar to us, not because we have studied him so much as adults, but because we were taught a song about him as children. We are going to look at what we know of Zacchaeus, one of my favorite men in the Bible.

In Luke 13:22 we read that Jesus traveled through Galilee, going through cities and villages on His last journey to Jerusalem and teaching as He went. The next few chapters of Luke detail His travels. At this time large crowds followed Him to hear His words and to see Him perform miracles. In Luke 18, He encountered the rich young ruler who asked, "What shall I do to inherit eternal life?" (v. 18). When Jesus admonished him to sell all he possessed and distribute it to the poor, the man went away very sad, for he was rich (v. 23).

Then in Luke 18:35 Jesus passed by a blind man, who called out to him. Mark tells us his name was Bartimaeus (Mark 10:46). When Jesus questioned him closer, Bartimaeus said he wanted to regain his sight, and Jesus immediately healed his blindness (Luke 18:41-43).

The next incident related for us involved Zacchaeus not long after Jesus entered Jericho (Luke 19:1). In New Testament times, Jericho was about 17 miles from Jerusalem, about a mile south of the site of Old Testament Jericho.[1] A wealthy and important city of Palestine, Jericho was under Roman authority during this time.

In Jericho lived a man named Zacchaeus. It seems odd that his name means "pure," for that is certainly not a word we would have used to describe him after first meeting him. We know he was a Jew because Zacchaeus is a Jewish name and later Jesus called him "a son of Abraham" (Luke 19:9).

Zacchaeus was a chief tax collector (Luke 19:2). Tax collectors were Jews who worked for the foreign government – the hated Romans – gathering taxes. We would call them government employees. Zacchaeus seemed to be the supervisor of this district. As the chief tax collector, he probably had tax collectors working under him. Like IRS workers today, these tax gatherers were not popular in the public eye. The reason for this attitude is that most of them were crooks. The tax gatherer could extort for his own benefit more money than was due, and the Romans didn't care. They could make you pay $100 when you only owed $50 and pocket the other $50. Tax collectors were so detested that the very name "publican" or "tax gatherer" was commonly associated with the word "sinner" (Matthew 9:10-11). The fact that Zacchaeus is said to have been rich makes us suspect he took more from the common people than he should have. Why are we specifically told that Zacchaeus was rich? Remember, it was not too long before this that Jesus met the rich young ruler who turned away from the Lord. This encounter may be in contrast to that sad confrontation.

Zacchaeus had heard of Jesus; he wanted to see who Jesus was and to learn more about Him. Because Jesus had recently restored the sight of Bartimaeus, now throngs of people crowded Jesus wherever He went. The roads may have also been crowded with people going to Jerusalem for the Passover. And Zacchaeus was short or, as some would say, vertically challenged. This is where I empathize with Zacchaeus. At "five feet short," I have been to parades or in groups where I could not see a thing. *The Bible Background Commentary* indicates that for Zacchaeus to have been considered short by ancient Mediterranean standards, he would have been less than five feet tall.[2] Likely, he was no taller than me. Certainly, he was unable to see over the people. But Zacchaeus was not only short; he was also smart, quick and agile.

The Bible Exposition Commentary explains it would have been unusual in the Eastern part of the world for a man to run, especially a wealthy government official, for it would have seemed undignified.[3] But run he did. He put aside his pride, ran ahead of the crowd, and climbed into a sycamore tree in order to get a height advantage. What is called the sycamore tree in the Scriptures is different from the North American sycamore or the European-Asian sycamore maple. Instead, it is related to the fig tree and is an easy tree to climb. Because Jericho was such a prosperous city, there were probably spacious villas and parks nearby with trees handy.

Zacchaeus was in for a big surprise. When Jesus walked by, not only did He know somebody was up in the tree but He called Zacchaeus by name! We are reminded of our Good Shepherd who calls His flock by name: "To him the doorkeeper opens, and the sheep hear his voice; and he calls his own sheep by name and leads them out" (John 10:3).

The Jews normally considered the ability to know the name of someone you had never met to be the sort of thing only a prophet could do. Imagine the shock if someone with a large following singled you out and called you by name.

Talking to Zacchaeus was not all Jesus did; He also invited Himself to Zacchaeus's home. Much like today, people then normally didn't invite themselves to someone's home for a meal. To have Jesus eat a meal in his home was a great honor for Zacchaeus. The original language translated "I must stay at your house" signifies to dwell, remain or tarry.[4] One can assume that Jesus spent the night in the house of Zacchaeus and then continued on His journey the next day.

Zacchaeus did not wait to be asked twice. Without delay he climbed down out of the tree while everyone else started to grumble and criticize. The Easy-to-Read Version says: "Everyone saw this. They began to complain, 'Look at the kind of man Jesus is staying with. Zacchaeus is a sinner!'" (Luke 19:7). All the tax collectors were regarded as great sinners, and the "chief publican" was regarded as especially wicked. The crowds simply could not fathom why Jesus would choose this particular man, this sinner, to be His host; and they did not approve, not one little bit.

But Zacchaeus listened to the Lord anyway and took Jesus to his home. Luke tells us Zacchaeus "received Him joyfully" (Luke 19:6). *The Greek-Hebrew Dictionary* tells us that phrase means to admit under one's roof or to entertain hospitably.[5]

Then the most amazing, unbelievable, wonderful change in the attitude of Zacchaeus is described for us: "Then Zacchaeus stood and said to the Lord, 'Look, Lord, I give half of my goods to the poor; and if I have taken anything from anyone by false accusation, I restore fourfold'" (Luke 19:8).

Scripture is silent concerning what was said to bring about so great a change in his attitude. No doubt he heard and believed the Lord's teachings. Zacchaeus was willing to give up his ill-gotten riches in an effort to make amends. He wanted to make restitution to those he had wronged. He was willing to give half of his possessions to the poor and give back four times as much to anyone he had defrauded. His restitution goes far beyond the Law, which required fourfold or fivefold restitution only for stolen oxen and sheep, only if he slaughtered or sold them, and only if a sufficient number of people witnessed the act (Exodus 22:1). Roman law did require tax gatherers to make restitution if there was proof they had abused their power by oppressing the people, but here we see no proof offered. We see only Zacchaeus's desire to show the sincerity of his conversion.

Jamieson, Fausset, and Brown Commentary explains that the "if" in this verse – when Zacchaeus clarifies, "if I have taken anything from anyone" – is not meant to express any doubt of the fact, but only the difficulty of fixing it. They write that the meaning is "in so far as I have done this," I will give back.[6]

Zacchaeus must have thought he was seeking Jesus, but in reality, Jesus was seeking him. The Jews thought that being in the family of Abraham would save them, but that was not enough. They needed to seek to know Jesus, just as Zacchaeus sought to know Him. Zacchaeus was not saved because he promised to do good works; he was saved because he responded in faith to Jesus Christ. The restitution was only proof of a changed life.

So what is the significance of the story of Zacchaeus to us as adults (besides bringing some comfort to the vertically challenged of the world)?

What Lessons Do We Learn From Zacchaeus?

1. We should be willing to overcome our physical challenges to see Jesus.

Today we worship and study in air-conditioned buildings with padded pews and still have trouble attracting people to hear the words of Jesus. I wonder how many of us would be willing to climb a tree to hear His words. It was not Zacchaeus's fault that he was short; thankfully he did not let that hardship keep him from seeing Jesus.

2. We shouldn't let riches keep us from Jesus.

It is interesting that Zacchaeus joined the multitude trying to see Jesus in the first place. His mind was not completely engrossed by financial considerations. Attaining more money was not the most important goal in his life. Can you be rich and go to heaven? Absolutely. Riches are not an insurmountable barrier against following the Lord (Luke 18:27). Jesus proclaimed the gospel to the rich and poor alike. Riches can, however, make it more difficult to be faithful. We must not let riches or the desire for riches separate us from God.

> *And when Jesus saw that he became very sorrowful, He said, "How hard it is for those who have riches to enter the kingdom of God! For it is easier for a camel to go through the eye of a needle than for a rich man to enter the kingdom of God."*
> *(Luke 18:24-25)*

3. We should be willing to accept the truth when we hear it.

Zacchaeus was blessed to have personal instruction from Jesus, and whatever Jesus said, Zacchaeus accepted it completely. We don't see procrastination; we don't see hesitancy; we don't see disbelief. Zacchaeus was a man of authority, but he was willing to humble himself before the Savior.

4. We should be willing to make amends for our wrongs.

Making amends for Zacchaeus was not only about paying back the money. It was also about admitting to those who knew him that he had done wrong, which might have caused embarrassment. This probably would have included asking for their forgiveness in the process. He might have been laughed at; he might have made some people angry to learn he had cheated them; he might have gotten in trouble with the authorities. Zacchaeus was willing to chance all that in order to make things right.

I love the way Zacchaeus is characterized in *Willmington's Bible Handbook*: "Zacchaeus did not allow his sin, size, or silver to keep him from the Savior."[7] *The Bible Exposition Commentary* remarks: "When a day begins, you never know how it will end. For Zacchaeus, that day ended in joyful fellowship with the Son of God, for he was now a changed man with a new life."[8] Zacchaeus may have been short, but with Jesus he could feel 10 feet tall!

Let's Think About This

1. Zacchaeus did not let his short stature prevent him from seeing Jesus. What types of problems must people overcome today in order to follow Jesus?

2. Why did the multitudes care that Jesus went home with Zacchaeus?

3. Name faithful people in the Scriptures who were wealthy.

4. In what ways do riches make it harder to stay faithful?

5. What prevents people from accepting the truth when they hear it?

6. How hard is it to make amends for our sins? What is the answer for those sins we are unable to make right?

NATHANAEL:

Never Assume Anything

John 1:43-51; 21:2

Misspoken words can escape the lips of any one of us at any time. Many "bloopers" have even been attributed to celebrities over the years.

- Brooke Shields, during an interview: "Smoking kills. If you're killed, you've lost a very important part of your life."
- One of Washington D.C.'s former mayors, Marion Barry: "Outside of the killings, Washington has one of the lowest crime rates in the country."
- Jason Kidd, upon being drafted by the Dallas Mavericks: "We're going to turn this team around 360 degrees."
- Duffy Daugherty, football coach and sports analyst: "Not only is he ambidextrous, but he can throw with either hand."
- Bill Peterson, football coach: "Men, I want you just thinking of one word all season. One word and one word only – Super Bowl."

My granddaughter Amanda was at a soccer game with her family and wanted to get something to eat from the "confession" stand. Another time Amanda was pointing out my appliances to her brother Nathan: "This is the clothes dryer and this is the wetter."

Foot-in-mouth disease is described by Dictionary.com as "the habit of making inappropriate, insensitive, or imprudent statements," and it strikes more often than we like to admit. We say something totally inappropriate or make rash and thoughtless comments. We may use a wrong word or blurt out remarks that would be better left unsaid. A man named Nathanael did the same thing when he was first told about Jesus. Nathanael's story is found in the Gospel of John; his name occurs only in that book of the Bible.

I love what Ted Scheuermann and Paul Heidebrecht write about Nathanael in their book *Men Like Us*: "The first time Nathanael heard about Jesus, he did what many of us do regularly – speak without thinking first. He opened his mouth and said something stupid."[1] Since this happens to all of us, it is nice to know people have been misspeaking since biblical times. Our mouths go into action before our brains can kick into gear, and before we know it, something stupid pops out. A lot of times, when we hear it out loud, we know our words do not make sense, but it's too late. We have contracted foot-in-mouth disease.

At the beginning of His ministry, before He had even called His apostles, Jesus traveled to Galilee, where he called Philip to follow Him. Evidently, the men of Galilee had been stirred to faith, having first followed John the Baptist, and now they were ready to follow Jesus. In his excitement, the first thing Philip did was find his friend Nathanael to share with him the wonderful news that the Messiah had been found. Remember that the Jews had been waiting and watching for the Savior to come for many years; they had studied the prophecies and knew what was foretold about the Messiah. They believed the Messiah would come; it was just a matter of when, and now was that time. You know the feeling when something thrilling happens and you just can't wait to tell someone? Philip couldn't wait to tell his friend this life-changing, good news. He found Nathanael and excitedly identified Jesus from Nazareth, son of Joseph, as the long-awaited Messiah.

Nathanael was immediately skeptical – not of Jesus' lineage as the son of the carpenter Joseph but of His place of residence, Nazareth. Nathanael probably considered Nazareth an insignificant town, hardly the place where one would look to find the Redeemer of Israel. It was small, isolated and inaccessible. Nathanael said, "Can anything good come out of Nazareth?" (John 1:46). Can you hear the sarcasm in his voice as he asked that question? We might ask if anything good could come out of Podunk. Nazareth was considered unimportant; it was the boondocks of Galilee. Nathanael was ready to reject Jesus on this basis alone, but he obviously had jumped to a wrong conclusion and made an insensitive statement.

Fortunately for Nathanael, Philip was a wise man. He did not argue but instead advised Nathanael to come and see for himself. Philip might have gotten into an argument with Nathanael: "Of course good things come out of Nazareth! Who do you think you are to think otherwise?" We might have responded in that way. Instead Philip calmly invited Nathanael to check out the situation. Thankfully, Nathanael was willing to do that.

John 1:47 quotes Jesus as saying, "Behold, an Israelite indeed, in whom is no deceit!" This is the only time the word "Israelite" is used in the Gospels and one of only four times in the whole New Testament. It was obviously a compliment paid to this man whom Jesus had never met. Jesus knew Nathanael was worthy of being called an Israelite, a believer in the one true God.

> For he is not a Jew who is one outwardly, nor is circumcision that which is outward in the flesh; but he is a Jew who is one inwardly; and circumcision is that of the heart, in the Spirit, not in the letter; whose praise is not from men but from God. (Romans 2:28-29)

No deceit was found in Nathanael. The American Standard Version uses the word "guile" in place of "deceit." The Easy-to-Read Version declares, "This man coming is a true Israelite, one you can trust." Jesus truly saw Nathanael's heart and recognized his honesty and integrity, characteristics valued by the psalmist in Psalm 32:2: "Blessed is the man to whom the LORD does not impute iniquity, and in whose spirit there is no deceit."

Nathanael was curious as to how Jesus knew anything about him. We would wonder that as well. Jesus saw Nathanael under the fig tree, but we are not told when that was. John writes that Jesus "said to him, 'Before Philip called you, when you were under the fig tree, I saw you'" (John 1:48). It could have been that day or a week earlier or any other time for all we know. The shade of a fig tree was a favorite place for study and prayer in hot weather, but we don't really know what Nathanael was doing under the fig tree.[2] Some sources claim he was meditating or praying, but when the Scriptures do not say so specifically, we must not take such liberties. The verse simply says Jesus saw him when he was under the fig tree before Philip called him.

Nathanael immediately recognized that Jesus had unique knowledge of him and He must truly be the Messiah, for only the Messiah could have had information such as this. Nathanael confessed his belief without hesitation, calling Him Rabbi, meaning "my teacher" (John 1:49). Rabbi was a title of great dignity used by the Jews to show honor and respect to a teacher of the Law. What a huge change from "Can anything good come out of Nazareth?" to "Rabbi, You are the Son of God!" (vv. 46, 49). When Nathanael was in the presence of Jesus, all doubts were swept away.

John 1:51 is, in part, a quotation from Genesis 28:12, when Jacob had his dream about the ladder to heaven with angels ascending and descending. Jesus connects heaven and earth; He is the "ladder" bridging the gulf between God and man. Jesus stated that Nathanael would see even greater things regarding Jesus as the mediator between heaven and earth, God and men.

The only other time we read of Nathanael is in John 21:2, where we are told he was a native of Cana in Galilee. As before, he was in the company of apostles: Peter, Thomas, the sons of Zebedee and two other unnamed disciples. At the Sea of Tiberias, which was another name for the Sea of Galilee, Nathanael was blessed to be one of those to whom the Lord showed Himself after His resurrection.

It is a little puzzling to many as to why Nathanael's name is absent from the lists of apostles. He talked with Jesus at the time when He called several of the apostles. Obviously he was a good man and a follower of Jesus. The theory is, although it can't be directly proven from the Scriptures, that Nathanael and Bartholomew were the same person. Bible reference books such as *Fausset's Bible Dictionary* give reasons why it is believed they are the same man. All we know about Bartholomew is that he was an apostle, and his name meant son of Tolmai, so it is possible that Nathanael was his given name. The book of John, which mentions Nathanael twice, never includes the name Bartholomew. Matthew, Mark and Luke all speak of Bartholomew but never of Nathanael. We might also mention that several of the apostles had two names – Matthew Levi, Simon Peter, Judas Iscariot and Thaddaeus Lebbaeus. It is entirely possible that Nathanael Bartholomew was his full name, but we are not certain.

What Lessons Do We Learn From Nathanael?

1. We should bring our friends to Jesus.

Philip had wonderful news to share, and he wanted to tell his friend Nathanael. Perhaps they had previously heard rumors regarding Jesus and discussed the amazing possibility that He might really be the Messiah. Now Philip was convinced that Jesus was the One Moses and the prophets had written about. Just as Andrew brought Peter to Jesus (John 1:40-41), Philip found Nathanael to lead him to Jesus. We have the wonderful news of our Savior, Jesus Christ. We should be standing on the rooftops and shouting it to the world! Surely, sharing this news with friends we love should be a joy.

And daily in the temple, and in every house, they did not cease teaching and preaching Jesus as the Christ. (Acts 5:42)

2. Don't jump to conclusions.

Nathanael immediately reacted with cynicism to the news about the Messiah. We can almost hear his derisive tone when he said, "Where? Nazareth? Nothing good can come out of Nazareth." Unfortunately we also often base our assumptions on opinions, incorrect information, prejudices, appearances and previous experiences instead of solely looking for the truth. In our spiritual lives, jumping to conclusions is dangerous. We may conclude some are not worthy of hearing the gospel because of their past; we may not want to teach others because we assume they will not listen.

Judge not, that you be not judged. For with what judgment you judge, you will be judged; and with the measure you use, it will be measured back to you. And why do you look at the speck in your brother's eye, but do not consider the plank in your own eye? Or how can you say to your brother, "Let me remove the speck from your eye"; and look, a plank is in your own eye? Hypocrite! First remove the plank from your own eye, and then you will see clearly to remove the speck from your brother's eye. (Matthew 7:1-5)

3. Don't be afraid to change your mind.

When confronted with the truth, Nathanael quickly erased any problems with Nazareth from his thinking and worshiped Jesus. If our beliefs are wrong, we need to be willing to admit that and change our views. If we are convicted of sin in our hearts, we must follow Nathanael's example and turn to Jesus. That is the true meaning of conversion.

4. Remember Jesus knows your true self.

You cannot deceive Jesus. He knew Nathanael's heart, and He knows our hearts. He plainly stated this in Luke 16:15: "You are those who justify yourselves before men, but God knows your hearts. For what is highly esteemed among men is an abomination in the sight of God."

How does that make you feel? Does it make you feel comfortable? Thankful? Afraid? Anxious? We must live in such a way that Jesus will be pleased when He sees our hearts.

5. When in the presence of Jesus, all doubts can be swept away.

How glorious is this thought! Staying in the presence of Jesus will help us to be strong and faithful in our walk as Christian women.

Let's Think About This

1. What suggestions do you have for avoiding "foot-in-mouth" disease?

2. Why do you suppose Nathanael thought nothing good could come out of Nazareth?

3. Do we talk to our friends about Jesus? If not, why not? Are we afraid of their reactions?

4. What is the danger of jumping to conclusions regarding spiritual matters?

5. What prevents us from changing our minds? Why is this so hard?

6. Is it harder to change our minds when it comes to religion than in other areas of life? Why?

NICODEMUS:

Go to the Source

John 3:1-15; 7:45-52; 19:38-42

Late one night when my dad was out of town, my mother thought she heard a strange noise. My husband and I didn't live too far from them at the time so she called us. My husband, Wendell, bravely hurried to their house armed with the only weapon he could find – a baseball bat. Thankfully, no bad guy was there to test his skill with the bat. Some might say he was courageous, even heroic; others might call him foolish or reckless. Perhaps a man spends all his time teaching Bible studies. He is dedicated, some would say; others would accuse him of neglecting his family. If a mother refuses to let her children out of her sight, some would say she is overprotective, but she might also be thought of as a good parent.

The lessons we can learn from one Bible character depend, at least in part, on our perspective. To some, Nicodemus may seem like a coward, or he may seem to you like a good man searching for the truth.

While opinions on Nicodemus's character may vary, here's what we do know: he was an important Jewish leader who is mentioned only in the Gospel of John. Although the name Nicodemus was common among the Jews of the first century, he is the only man in the New Testament to bear that name.[1] He was a Pharisee, a member of the strict religious sect that followed the Mosaic Law to a T. He was also a member of the Sanhedrin, the body of chief priests, elders and scribes who governed Israel in New Testament times. Nicodemus knew the Law; he was educated in and dedicated to the Jewish religion. It could have been expected of such a man that he knew the Old Testament well indeed. As a teacher of Israel, he had a special responsibility for the religious instruction of the people of God.

The time was fairly early in the public ministry of Jesus. Nicodemus had obviously heard of Jesus and the amazing miracles He had performed. He recognized that Jesus was a teacher sent from God. One night, Nicodemus went to see Jesus (John 3:2). Here is where those different perspectives come in. Some people read this, even some Bible scholars, and are convinced he was a coward. Their theory is he went at night so his fellow Pharisees would not be aware of it and the rendezvous could remain a secret. He did not want to face their ridicule and contempt.

Others have a different view, believing he went at night to have a quiet conversation with Jesus. Maybe Nicodemus wanted a little one-on-one time with Jesus. Because Jesus was surrounded by crowds during the day, it was impossible to speak privately with Him. Perhaps Nicodemus was just too busy to go during the day, or maybe he was just being cautious, knowing how the other leaders felt about Jesus. What do you think? Was he prudent? Discreet? Afraid? It is even possible that Nicodemus was hesitant to stir things up until he knew what this Jesus man was all about.

Our perspective of why he went at night colors our overall opinion of him. If we think of him as cowardly, it will affect how we read the rest of his story. But if we view him as honestly searching for the truth, that will also shape what we learn from him. I like to think he was an honest man, seeking the truth about Jesus. He is the first Pharisee that we read about in Scripture who exhibited a kind attitude toward Jesus. The Sanhedrin as a whole was totally against this Man who ran the merchants out of the temple, which He claimed to be His Father's house (John 2:15-16). For Nicodemus to want to talk to Jesus at all was a big step. The Pharisees had already taken an open stand against Jesus and certainly would not have approved of Nicodemus not only meeting with Jesus but also admitting that He was a teacher sent from God (3:2). Even though he did meet Jesus at night, it was a courageous undertaking.

Although it was nighttime and He may have been tired from teaching all day, Jesus was willing to chat with Nicodemus. After Nicodemus admitted that Jesus was clearly a teacher from God, Jesus took the opportunity to explain how Nicodemus, too, could enter the kingdom of God: "Most assuredly, I say to you, unless one is born again, he cannot see the kingdom of God" (John 3:3).

Nicodemus obviously didn't understand the declaration from Jesus as he asked, "How can a man be born when he is old?" (John 3:4). How could he have grasped its significance? He had no frame of reference at this time to help him comprehend Jesus' meaning. Nicodemus took what Jesus said literally and assumed He referred to a physical birth. The fact that Nicodemus was a Pharisee related directly to the conversation Jesus had with him, for such a conversation would have been highly improbable with the sects of the Sadducees or Herodians. As a Pharisee, Nicodemus looked for a political kingdom under a political Messiah; he thought in physical terms. But Jesus spoke of a spiritual kingdom.

> Jesus answered, "Most assuredly, I say to you, unless one
> is born of water and the Spirit, he cannot enter the kingdom
> of God. That which is born of the flesh is flesh, and that
> which is born of the Spirit is spirit." (vv. 5-6)

To be born of water and the Spirit refers to the inward, spiritual change that must take place. As Albert Barnes stresses in his commentary, "born of water" in John 3:5 "evidently signified 'baptism.'"[2] Again, Nicodemus did not demonstrate any understanding.

Jesus continued to patiently teach Nicodemus the great truths of God's love. Nicodemus was privileged to personally hear the teachings of Jesus in a private, face-to-face interaction (John 3:7-21).

In John 7, Jesus was in Jerusalem during the Feast of Tabernacles or Booths. He taught in the temple and people were amazed by the words He spoke. Many people believed He was the Christ. Word got back to the Pharisees and priests that people actually said this man was the Messiah. The thought that the people might follow this newcomer with His claim of being sent by God upset the Jewish leaders. In an effort to put an end to His growing popularity, they sent some officers from the temple to arrest Jesus (v. 32), but the outcome was not what they anticipated.

The multitude did not stop them from making an arrest; instead, it was the very words that Jesus spoke that made them stop in their tracks (John 7:45-46). What a courageous act on the part of these policemen! Because they failed to arrest Him, they faced ridicule from their superiors:

Then the Pharisees answered them, "Are you also deceived? Have any of the rulers or the Pharisees believed in Him? But this crowd that does not know the law is accursed." (vv. 47-49)

The New Century Version reads, "So Jesus has fooled you also!" The implication was that the religious leaders were too smart to believe in Him; only the riffraff, the common people, would believe such a thing. These very men, those trained in the Law and the prophets, should have been the first ones to acknowledge Jesus as the Messiah, but they failed to accept the evidence right in front of their eyes. Perhaps they would have ordered the temple guards to return and bring Jesus to them, but they heard one of their own raise an objection. Nicodemus did not keep quiet; he spoke up.

Nicodemus raised a point of order in favor of Jesus: "Does our law judge a man before it hears him and knows what he is doing?" (John 7:51). Although we are not given the exact law Nicodemus was referencing, every man deserved his day in court just as in our judicial system today. Nicodemus didn't come right out and admit he was a believer, but certainly compared to the other Pharisees, he took up for Jesus, and like the temple police, he was mocked for it.

The other religious leaders accused Nicodemus of being a follower of the Man from Galilee with the implication that it was a bad thing (John 7:52). We can almost hear the derision in their voices. In an effort to take a further jab at Jesus, they made a rash and wrong statement that no prophet ever came from Galilee. They should have remembered that Jonah, Elijah and Micah were all faithful prophets out of Galilee. The Pharisees uttered anything they could against Jesus whether it was correct or not. After arguing with Nicodemus, they gave up and went home.

The last we read of Nicodemus is after the crucifixion of Jesus. After a crucifixion, the body would probably have been taken outside the city and thrown on the garbage heap unless family or a powerful patron interceded for the body. In Judaism, burying the dead was an important act of love; being left unburied was too horrible to be permitted, even for criminals.³ Joseph of Arimathea, another believer, asked for and was granted permission to take the body of Jesus for burial (John 19:38). Nicodemus, described as the one "who at first came to Jesus by night" (v. 39), joined Joseph as they prepared the body of Jesus for burial according to Jewish customs. Nicodemus provided 75 pounds of myrrh and aloes, probably placed within the linen used to wrap the body. The large amount of the spices may indicate the wealth of Nicodemus but certainly shows his dedication to Jesus (vv. 40-42).

We learn in Mark that Joseph was also a member of the Sanhedrin (Mark 15:43). Notice that John 19:38 discloses that Joseph was a secret disciple for fear of the Jews, but it doesn't say this about Nicodemus. Do you suppose this is where people get the idea that Nicodemus was previously afraid to come to Jesus during the day? Together, Joseph and Nicodemus placed the body in a tomb not yet used. *Matthew Henry's Commentary* explains that Jesus was buried in a new tomb so it could not be said that it was not He, but some other who rose from the dead.⁴

The book of Matthew tells us that it was Joseph's own tomb (Matthew 27:60). Evidently Joseph was a rich man, for he owned his tomb and was able to approach Pilate for the body. Thus was the prophecy in Isaiah 53:9 fulfilled regarding Jesus' death: "And they made His grave with the wicked – but with the rich at His death, because He had done no violence, nor was any deceit in His mouth."

Remember the Sabbath was coming at sundown, and no one was to prepare a body for burial on that day as that would have been considered working on the Sabbath. It was imperative they prepare the body quickly and the tomb be close at hand.

We are not told in Scripture what happened to Nicodemus after the burial of Jesus, but Christian tradition tells us Nicodemus was baptized by Peter and John. He is alleged to have suffered persecution from the Jews, "lost his membership in the Sanhedrin, and was forced to leave Jerusalem because of his Christian faith."⁵ Some historians even claim he was martyred for his faith.

What Lessons Do We Learn From Nicodemus?

1. Don't let a difficult situation keep you from Jesus.

Even if Nicodemus really did go to see Jesus at night out of fear, the important lesson for us is that he went. He did not let the late hour or the fear of his companions in the Sanhedrin keep him from Jesus. Sometimes it's hard for us to show that we are Christians. Maybe our family makes it difficult for us to be faithful; our husbands may put a stumbling block in our paths; perhaps it is our jobs or our friends who try to prevent us from living the Christian life. Nicodemus struggled with his circumstances, but in the end, he took his stand for Jesus.

2. If you are struggling with questions or doubts, go to the source.

Nicodemus seems to have sincerely wanted to know the truth; therefore, he went directly to Jesus for answers. What a wonderful privilege we have been given to be able to go to the Scriptures to hear the words of Jesus for ourselves. We must not depend solely on a minister or a teacher or anyone else to tell us the truth, because they may lead us astray. If we go directly to the Bible and study for ourselves, we know we are learning the truth.

3. Nicodemus did what he could.

First, he spoke up for Jesus; then he buried Him. Unlike other Jewish religious leaders, Nicodemus did not allow the scorn of his peers to keep him from following Christ. If you have the opportunity as Nicodemus did among the members of the Sanhedrin, speak up for Jesus. Every time you proclaim Jesus, you will be glad you did.

> Therefore whoever confesses Me before men, him I will also confess before My Father who is in heaven. (Matthew 10:32)

4. Continue your journey of faith in Christ.

We see a progression in the faith of Nicodemus. He was searching for the truth; then he spoke up for Christ; finally he showed his love for Christ in his actions. You may not feel like your spiritual life is where it should be, but don't give up; it is a journey. We must continue to let our faith develop, grow and mature until we are able to show our love for Christ in all we do.

Let's Think About This

1. Why do you think Nicodemus approached Jesus at night?

2. In what ways can we approach Jesus today? What kinds of situations keep people from going to Jesus?

3. Why do you think Nicodemus assisted with the burial of Jesus?

4. Are you surprised that the apostles did not return for the body of Jesus? What reasons might have kept them from approaching Pilate for permission to bury Him?

5. Who taught you as you began your Christian journey? What roadblocks, if any, have hindered your progression of faith?

THE MAN BORN BLIND:

A Miracle Made of Clay

John 8:59; 9

My husband, Wendell, and I had been to visit at the hospital one day and were getting in the car to leave. He had parked in the special parking place designated for ministers. A man came up and stopped us. He said he was traveling to Alabama and desperately needed money for gas. It's sometimes difficult to know whether to help someone in a situation like this. Wendell asked him a couple of questions and finally told him he could follow us to a gas station. When we got there, Wendell paid to fill up the man's car with gas. The man promised he would mail us a check when he got home, but, of course, we are still waiting for it. Wendell told him he would be happy if he would just attend worship at home. I am convinced the man targeted us for help because we were parked in that minister's parking spot. I suppose he thought he had a better chance of getting help from somebody whose job it is to be compassionate.

I suspect that the man in our study today did pretty much the same thing. When he needed help, he probably went to the place where religious people gathered, where people would hopefully be kinder and more willing to help. I would tell you the name of this man, but God did not tell us.

John relates an incident involving this man that happened in Jerusalem. Jesus had been teaching in the temple, but when He said to the

Jews "Most assuredly, I say to you, before Abraham was, I AM" (John 8:58), they became very upset and took up stones to throw at Him. Jesus went out of the temple to escape (v. 59). A very common place for beggars was around the temple in the hopes of receiving more alms there, and as Jesus had just left the temple, it makes sense that this man may have been close by.

This man had been blind since birth, and at that time becoming a beggar was the only profession available to him (John 9:1, 8). When Jesus saw the man, His disciples questioned the reason he was blind. They believed, as did many at that time, that suffering, including blindness, was often due to sin – either one's own sin or his parents' sin. Jesus patiently took the opportunity to explain to His disciples that neither this man nor his parents had sinned (vv. 2-5). Jesus then graciously turned His attention to the beggar. The man was accustomed to hearing voices of people around him; some of those voices may even have been accusatory or critical of him. But suddenly he heard a new voice, a voice that would change his life forever.

Jesus spat on the ground and made clay with the saliva. With the clay, He anointed the eyes of the blind man (John 9:6-7). Those of us who are mothers know how a little spit can clean a face; but at that time spittle was considered vulgar and gross.[1] We can only imagine what this man thought as Jesus put mud on his eyes. Remember he could not see what Jesus was doing. I wonder if Jesus explained about the clay as He smeared it on the man's eyes.

Only occasionally did Jesus use any external props in a miracle. Why do you suppose He did now? Matthew Henry writes in his commentary that it would "magnify his power in making a blind man to see by that method which one would think more likely to make a seeing man blind." He adds, "Daubing clay on the eyes would close them up, but never open them."[2]

The blind man was then given instructions, and he did exactly what Jesus commanded. He went to the pool of Siloam, feeling his way, maybe with the help of a passer-by. He washed the clay off his eyes with the cool water, and when he did, he saw the sparkling blue water in the pool. He could see! We say that so simply, but for the first time in this grown man's life, he could see what was going on around him. I doubt we can understand the full impact of seeing the world for the first time.

This sermon illustration offers a more detailed understanding of how this man must have felt seeing for the first time:

> *For 51 years Bob Edens was blind. He couldn't see a thing.*
> *His world was a black hall of sounds and smells. He felt his*
> *way through five decades of darkness. And then, he could see.*
> *A skilled surgeon performed a complicated operation and, for the*
> *first time, Bob Edens had sight. He found it overwhelming.*
> *"I never would have dreamed that yellow is so ... yellow," he*
> *exclaimed. "I don't have the words. I am amazed by yellow. But*
> *red is my favorite color. I just can't believe red. I can see the shape*
> *of the moon – and I like nothing better than seeing a jet plane flying*
> *across the sky leaving a vapor trail. And of course, sunrises and*
> *sunsets. And at night I look at the stars in the sky and the flashing*
> *light. You could never know how wonderful everything is."* [3]

We are not grateful enough for the blessing of sight.

You would think this man being given sight by Jesus would have been cause for celebration among his friends and neighbors, but sadly, this was not the case. The man returned to the place where he met Jesus. When the people there saw him, they could not believe what was before their eyes, saying, "This can't be him!" (cf. John 9:8-9). Here was the man they had passed by for years as he begged, totally blind, and now he could see. What a shock! Those blind from birth were not known to recover their sight. The people had trouble believing it was really the same man. Do you suppose they had never really looked closely at this beggar? Maybe they had just looked right past him previously. Finally, he settled the matter with the words, "I am he" (v. 9). Then, of course, they pushed him for details; they wanted to know how this happened. He could only tell them the basic facts: the Man called Jesus made clay, anointed his eyes and told him to wash. That was all he knew.

The man struggled physically before; now he struggled because of lack of knowledge. He knew a Man named Jesus gave him sight, but keep in mind, he did not even see Jesus because he was still blind at the time Jesus was there. The man did not know how Jesus had healed him, and he did not know where Jesus had gone after the miraculous healing.

Because the people did not really know what to believe, they deemed it prudent to take the matter before the Pharisees, the spiritual leaders of the day. When the Pharisees heard the story, they were not happy at all. They were upset for two reasons: (1) because they could not explain the miracle and (2) because it took place on the Sabbath. The Jews were not supposed to work on the Sabbath, and the Pharisees considered healing to be work. The religious leaders had come up with 39 classes of work forbidden on the Sabbath. God did not specify these – men did. One of the categories was kneading, as in working with dough, and it probably included clay.[4] The fact that Jesus did not keep the Sabbath according to their laws made the Pharisees even more irritated. So they asked the man what happened, and after he told them the same facts, they asked, "What do you say about Jesus?" Now he answered, "He is a prophet" (John 9:17). Do you see his struggle becoming a little less? First, he referred to the Man called Jesus; then he pronounced Him to be a prophet.

The Pharisees asked the man's parents to explain how their son could now see, but they were too intimidated to answer. They did not want to be thrown out of the synagogue, and this might very well have happened if they had admitted a belief in Jesus. The parents referred them back to their son, who was, after all, an adult who could answer questions for himself (John 9:18-23).

This healed man reiterated the only thing he knew: "though I was blind, now I see" (John 9:25). When the Jews persisted with their inter-rogation, he answered them again, "I told you already.… Do you also want to become His disciples?" (v. 27). He began to get a little bolder as he struggled to understand who Jesus really was.

He had come to the realization that Jesus was from God, and he was now courageous enough to say so. Even in light of their reproach and intimidation, he stuck to his guns. As a result, he was cast out of the synagogue by the Jewish leaders (John 9:34), which was a really big deal. When Jesus was teaching in Jerusalem, even many of the rulers believed in Him, but they didn't have the courage to confess that belief for fear of this very thing.

Nevertheless even among the rulers many believed in Him, but because of the Pharisees they did not confess Him, lest they should be put out of the synagogue; for they loved the praise of men more than the praise of God. (John 12:42-43)

Now our man who once was blind was dejected and discouraged. This day started out so wondrously with him having his sight provided to him, and now people were being hateful to him, even throwing him out of the place of worship. He must have felt like he was on a roller coaster ride. But his day changed again when Jesus found him.

In Agatha Christie's mysteries, the detective Hercule Poirot always wanted to use his brain cells when trying to figure something out. You can almost see the brain cells working in this man who once was blind as he tried to figure out who Jesus was. After he was thrown out of the temple, Jesus found him and asked, "Do you believe in the Son of God?" (John 9:35). The man's honest answer was "Who is He, Lord, that I may believe in Him?" (v. 36). He wanted to believe; he just did not know who or how.

Jesus disclosed to this man that, with his new sight, he had seen the Son of God and He was the one who talked with him now (John 9:37). When presented with the truth, the man immediately acknowledged his belief and worshiped Jesus. He had no doubt; his struggle was over. He progressed from knowing Jesus as a man, to a prophet, to a prophet from God, to the Son of God. And Jesus – instead of saying, "Why didn't you know who I am?" or "Why didn't you tell the Pharisees who I am?" – helped this man develop his faith and discover for himself the truth of Jesus' identity.

It is comforting to know that Jesus helped people who struggled with both physical and spiritual hardships. When we struggle with our faith, Jesus can help us too. He can help us as our faith increases. In Mark we read of a boy possessed with a spirit; as a result of the demon, he evidently had what we would call seizures. His father brought the boy to the disciples of Jesus, but no one could cast out this spirit (Mark 9:17-29). It seems the apostles' faith had not matured to the point that they could heal this child; they needed to progress in their faith.

> *And the apostles said to the LORD, "Increase our faith."*
> *So the LORD said, "If you have faith as a mustard seed,*
> *you can say to this mulberry tree, 'Be pulled up by the roots*
> *and be planted in the sea,' and it would obey you." (Luke 17:5-6)*

Even the apostles recognized their need for their faith to be increased. If we are not where we long to be spiritually, if we are blind and searching in some aspects of our faith, we must also strive to grow and mature as Christians.

What Lessons Do We Learn From the Man Born Blind?

1. We should do good as we pass by.

What an example Jesus set for us! In the end of John 8, the Jews were trying to stone Jesus, and He chose to escape from them. Still Jesus took the time, as He passed by this man who was born blind, to help him. He did not just see him and walk on by as the priest and Levite did in the parable of the good Samaritan (Luke 10:30-37). Jesus saw him and stopped to heal him, evidently without being asked.

We need to be on the lookout for opportunities to do good every day. Matthew Henry notes: "He did not defer it till he could do it either more privately, for his greater safety, or more publicly, for his greater honour, or till the sabbath was past, when it would give less offence."[5] Jesus saw a need, and He responded to it. Jesus took every opportunity to do good and so should we.

2. Maturing in our faith is a process.

We may not be to the point of being a "full-grown" Christian, but we can continue to mature in faith in Jesus Christ. If we continue to feed on the Word, spend time in fellowship with our brothers and sisters in Christ, and devote ourselves to prayer, we will see progress in our spiritual growth.

> *But grow in the grace and knowledge of our*
> *LORD and Savior Jesus Christ. (2 Peter 3:18)*

3. It takes courage to stand up for Jesus.

This blind man was a beggar when Jesus came upon him. He was not accustomed even to speaking with the leaders of the synagogue, much less contradicting them. But he bravely stood his ground when they tried to get him to speak badly of the One who had miraculously given him his sight; he refused to back down as he defended this Man to whom he owed so much. Christians today are being attacked more often as unbelievers try to get us to back down from our faith. In some countries, Christians have even been put to death merely for declaring their faith. Our prayers should be for courage to stand strong in the face of adversity.

Be of good courage, and He shall strengthen your heart,
all you who hope in the Lord. (Psalm 31:24)

4. When we believe, we will worship.

I love what the man did immediately after confessing his belief in Jesus – he worshiped. This man didn't say, "Yeah, I believe, but does that mean I have to attend worship services?" or "What about Sunday night? Does that count?" If we truly believe in God and His Son and realize how we have been blessed, we will desire to worship Him. No one should be able to prevent us from worshiping God. As faithful Christians, worship will be a priority in our lives.

5. The blindest of all are those who will not see.

Although the Pharisees did not face the challenges of physical blindness, they suffered from something with even greater repercussions: spiritual blindness. Of all people, these religious leaders should have accepted Christ as the Messiah; they were the ones who knew the prophecies and studied the Scriptures, but they refused to see the truth. We must always open our eyes to the truth of God.

When we think of this man whose sight was restored by Jesus, we are mindful of the greater blessing he received in learning the good news about Jesus. That same blessing is available for each one of us. As that old, familiar hymn so sweetly echoes, "I once was lost but now am found; was blind, but now I see."

Let's Think About This

1. What prevents us from taking advantage of opportunities to do good?

2. Name some specific things that have helped you mature in your faith.

3. In what circumstances are we called to stand up for Jesus?

4. How important is worship to the believer? Can you have a strong faith without worship?

THOMAS:

I Don't Believe It

John 11:1-16; 14:1-5; 20:1-9, 19-25; 21:1-6, 12-14

I recently saw two incredible men on television. One was Liu Wei, a 29-year-old man who won *China's Got Talent* in 2010, the Chinese equivalent of *America's Got Talent*. He won by playing the piano with his toes. His arms were amputated after he was electrocuted while playing hide-and-seek when he was 10 years old. Still, he taught himself to play piano. Remarkable is the only word to describe how someone could play the piano so beautifully by using his toes. It was hard to believe what I was hearing.

The other man was 33-year-old Nick Vujicic. He was born with no arms or legs. He now travels the world as a motivational speaker, telling humorous and inspirational stories to encourage people to be the best they can be. His hobbies include golfing, fishing and swimming. He demonstrates on his videos how he can kick a ball and use the one little foot that he has to answer a telephone. He truly is an inspiration.

Some things in this life are just so amazing that they are hard to believe. The man in our study experienced this same feeling. You are familiar with him, the apostle Thomas. Unfortunately, you may also be familiar with his nickname: "Doubting Thomas." Maybe some of us have never had any doubts about the existence of God or our faith in Jesus, but for others of us there are occasions in our lives when it may be difficult to believe.

We know very little about Thomas. The first we read of him is in both Matthew and Mark when his name is listed among those chosen to be apostles. We are not told anything about his background, his hometown or his occupation; we are told nothing except that he was picked to be an apostle. His work for the Lord as an apostle is not spelled out for us either. We do know that he was also called Didymus, the Greek word for "twin" (John 11:16).[1]

Jesus received word that his friend Lazarus was sick, and after a period of two days, He determined to go to him in Bethany. His disciples reminded Him that the Jews in that area were trying to kill Him, and it would be crazy to go back because it would be very dangerous (John 11:8). Of course, Jesus knew that, but after some discussion, Jesus said they would go anyway.

"Then Thomas, who is called the Twin, said to his fellow disciples, 'Let us also go, that we may die with Him'" (John 11:16). This was the first time the Bible records Thomas speaking. Thomas could see that the Lord was determined to go, but that did not make the threat from the Jews any less substantial. Thomas said, "We will go even if we die there." What does this statement tell us about him? The devotion of Thomas to his Master proved stronger than his fear of death. His faith in Jesus and loyalty to Him could not be questioned. Thomas knew fully the cost of following Jesus.

Doctors often advise patients of the risks and benefits of a particular procedure or of not having treatment for a serious condition. When I worked as a medical transcriptionist, the doctor would sometimes dictate: "The patient understands the risks and is willing to take them." Thomas understood the risks of going to Bethany, but he was willing to take those risks to follow Jesus. He encouraged the other disciples to follow this path as well.

The next time we see Thomas is in the upper room on the occasion of the Last Supper. Jesus had told His apostles that He was going to the Father, but they were clearly confused and did not understand that He had made reference to His death. Much of what Jesus said must have sounded like a riddle to them. His followers did not have the advantage of hindsight as we do now.

Let not your heart be troubled; you believe in God, believe also in Me.
In My Father's house are many mansions; if it were not so, I would
have told you. I go to prepare a place for you. And if I go and prepare a
place for you, I will come again and receive you to Myself; that where
I am, there you may be also. And where I go you know, and
the way you know. (John 14:1-4)

Most of us have been taught all our lives that Jesus was talking about heaven, but if we didn't know that and were hearing it for the first time, we might have thought he was going to Bethany or Nazareth. Disciples often asked their rabbis or teachers questions to clarify their teachings. Thomas was very matter-of-fact in his approach to Jesus; he did not beat around the bush. A lot of times we would be better off if we would just say what we mean. Thomas said, "Lord, we do not know where You are going, and how can we know the way?" (John 14:5). It almost sounded like a plea for further explanation. Thomas wanted to understand, but he didn't. To that request, Jesus gave His familiar answer: "I am the way, the truth, and the life" (v. 6). Jesus continued teaching His apostles, trying to prepare them for what was coming, but they still had trouble comprehending.

Thomas was an apostle, a firm believer in Jesus; he was ready to die for Him if necessary, but then it all fell apart. Jesus, the Son of God, the Messiah that the disciples fully expected to take His place over an earthly kingdom, was killed on a cross as if He were a common criminal. It is important we understand how the apostles felt. All of Thomas's hopes and dreams, all of his work for the last three years, everything he believed in was nailed to that cross. What a disappointment! What a letdown! What hurt he must have felt! Have you ever been hurt so deeply you just wanted to withdraw from humanity? You didn't want to see anybody or be strong for anybody else; you just wanted to suffer in your own way. Thomas and the other disciples were all feeling this sting of despair.

The disciples gathered on the Sunday after the Friday when Jesus had been crucified. They were in a room with the doors shut for fear of the Jews. It is no wonder they were afraid because the Jewish leaders had just spearheaded the crucifixion of Jesus. *The IVP Bible Background*

Commentary states that proper residences were equipped with bolts and locks that would prevent anyone from entering.[2] But suddenly, even despite closed doors, the resurrected Jesus stood before them. Jesus spoke to them with the standard Jewish greeting, "Peace be with you" (John 20:19). Then He showed them the wounds in His hands and His side to prove that He was the same Jesus who died.

This was the first encounter between Jesus and His disciples after His resurrection from the grave. For some unknown reason, Thomas was not there. Why were the other disciples able to believe that Jesus was alive? They saw Jesus for themselves; they heard Him talk; they may have even touched Him. They believed Jesus was alive, and they told Thomas, "Hey, Tom, guess who we saw!" But Thomas could not get the vision of Christ on the cross out of his mind. He knew Jesus had died. Just as Nathanael had been cynical, Thomas was doubtful. We have greatly criticized him for his attitude, but is he really so different from the other disciples? When Mary Magdalene ran to them and told them the tomb was empty, they did not take her word for it. They had to see for themselves (John 20:1-9). Thomas was asked to believe Jesus had come back from the dead and suddenly appeared in a room behind a closed door. Do you think it was just so wondrous that he couldn't believe it? Maybe he felt the same as people who are told they just won a big prize. They often say, "I just can't believe it!" Maybe he couldn't believe it either.

Clarence Macartney is quoted in the book *Growing Deep in the Christian Life* by Charles Swindoll:

> *This is the deepest doubt of all, the doubt born of sorrow; that is, the doubt which rises out of the experience of our lives. The doubt of Thomas was not that of quibbler or a cold-blooded student; it was the doubt of a man who had lost his LORD and Master. Sorrow had filled his heart.[3]*

Eight days later, the situation was the same – the disciples were gathered; the doors were shut. Do you think they were anxiously waiting to see if Jesus appeared again? I imagine you could have felt the tension in the room. Then, just as before, Jesus was present with them in the room, but this time Thomas was also in attendance. It speaks well of

Thomas that he was there with the other disciples. He did not say, "You are all crazy. I am not having anything else to do with you." Thomas was there in that same room with the others.

Earlier Thomas had expressed his reluctance to believe. Even though Jesus had not been present at that time, He was aware of the doubts of Thomas. Jesus turned to Thomas and offered to let him touch Him so he could believe (John 20:26-29). Did Thomas touch Jesus? We are not certain. Jesus said that because Thomas saw, he believed; Jesus did not say because he touched Him, he believed.

The effect on Thomas was immediate. Thomas said, "My Lord and my God!" (John 20:28). This was one of the strongest affirmations of faith in Jesus we have thus far in the Scriptures. Thomas no longer had any doubts at all. Now that he had seen Jesus for himself, just as the rest of the apostles had, he too believed. He went from being "Doubting Thomas" back to "Thomas the Believer." Jesus did not condemn Thomas for hesitating to believe; He helped lead him to the truth.

Some of the disciples, including Thomas, saw Jesus again when they were out fishing (John 21:1-6). Although they did not recognize Him at first, the disciples eventually realized this was Jesus. They rowed to shore where Jesus gave them bread and fish to eat (vv. 12-14).

In Acts 1:9-11 we are told that the apostles were privileged to see Jesus ascend back to heaven. Then Thomas and the other apostles gathered as instructed in Jerusalem to await the Holy Spirit (vv. 13-14).

Thomas is called a doubter, but he was also a believer. Do you know people who always look for reasons to doubt? They come up with Bible questions that have no apparent answers; they question why God does the things He does instead of trusting Him. Thomas wasn't one who tried not to believe or looked for reasons to doubt. Rather, he wanted to believe, to be able to put the hurt of losing Jesus behind him. Thankfully, he is set before us as a faithful follower of Christ.

What Lessons Do We Learn From Thomas?

1. We must be willing to sacrifice as we follow Jesus.

When Thomas saw what he needed to do, nothing held him back.

He was willing to go with Jesus to Bethany even though it might have meant death. This certainly sounds like he had faith, and it was a pretty strong faith at that. This makes me think about how petty our sacrifices are that we make in the Lord's service. We may miss a television show we wanted to watch because we are making a visit; we may have to stay up late to cook a dish for someone who is ill; we may get tired because we are working on a benevolence project. But Thomas was willing to die with Jesus. In comparison, our sacrifices seem pretty small.

2. We must not let our struggles and disappointments overwhelm us.

When we are facing hard times, we must not leave God out of our lives. I have known people who were faced with difficulties and decided God was not helping so they just left God completely. We may be disappointed over how another Christian treats us, or we may wonder why God allows us to suffer, but we must not let those things pull us away from God. We must continue to believe and trust in Him. Remember that even though Thomas was devastated after the death of Jesus, he never gave up; he was still in that room awaiting Jesus' second visit.

3. We must not let one weak moment in our lives define us.

The Bible never refers to Thomas as "Doubting Thomas." His moment of doubt is described, but it is one moment, only one, and he moved quickly beyond it. His identity, despite our perception and portrayal of him, is not rooted in that moment. Think about your own life. At some time you have said something you regretted or done something you wished you could take back. We all have. Do you want that sin to be the one thing that defines your life? We can rise above our doubts, our mistakes and our sins. We must not let the times we fail become who we are. We must not let one weak moment set the tone for our entire lives.

4. God will help us in our struggle to have faith.

How kind of Jesus to have appeared in that room the second time when Thomas was present! How thoughtful to offer Thomas the opportunity to touch His wounds! Jesus knew Thomas was struggling at that point, and He was willing to help him renew his faith. He understood what Thomas was going through. God will help us as well, but just as

Thomas did his part by being present in that room, we have to do our part by being open to God's comfort and teaching in His Word.

We all walk through storms of life on this earth. Some of us question, "Why me, Lord?" Some of us lose faith. Some of us struggle. Like Thomas, we must continue to want to believe, to search for the truth, and to be ready to listen to God when He talks to us through His Word.

Let's Think About This

1. Think of a time when you had doubts. How did you overcome them?

2. When Thomas had trouble believing Jesus had appeared to the other apostles, do you think Thomas thought they were lying? Hallucinating? Confused?

3. Is faith that has overcome doubt sometimes stronger than that which has never doubted?

4. Name other people in the Scriptures who overcame bad times and were ultimately faithful to God.

BARNABAS:

A Friend of Many

Acts 4:32-37; 9:26-27; 11:22-24

The Little League ballplayers dressed in blue uniforms thought they would win the game. Their players were better hitters, faster runners and more experienced catchers. They played hard, but so did the other team, and the final score was a tie. As they walked off the field, I overheard one father as he encouraged his disappointed son: "Isn't that great? The first tie of the season, and you got to be a part of it."

Everyone needs encouragement and recognition, but one little boy made it clear that he wanted positive feedback when he said to his father: "Let's play darts. I'll throw and you say 'Wonderful!'"[1] As Will Rogers said, "We can't all be heroes because somebody has to sit on the curb and clap as they go by." This poem, by William Arthur Ward, illustrates the importance of encouragement:

> *Flatter me, and I may not believe you.*
> *Criticize me, and I may not like you.*
> *Ignore me, and I may not forgive you.*
> *Encourage me, and I will not forget you.*[2]

The first Christians had their own benevolent program. They contributed to a common fund, and then each person was given what was needed (Acts 4:32-35). No one suffered from hunger or want. *The IVP Bible Background Commentary* describes it this way: "The outpouring of

God's Spirit here leads not only to miracles and inspired verbal witness but also to actively caring for one another and sharing possessions."[3] Barnabas was one who generously sold a field and gave the money to the apostles to be used for the Christians gathered there.

> *And Joses, who was also named Barnabas by the apostles (which is translated Son of Encouragement), a Levite of the country of Cyprus, having land, sold it, and brought the money and laid it at the apostles' feet. (Acts 4:36-37)*

Barnabas was a Jew from the tribe of Levi who was originally from the Greek island of Cyprus, not far from the coast of Israel. We remember that Levites in the Old Testament did not own land according to the law, but by Jesus' day, Levites were landowners although we are unsure whether the land he sold was in Cyprus or in the area of Jerusalem.[4]

We know this man as Barnabas, but his name was Joses or Joseph. The apostles added the name Barnabas, meaning "Son of Encouragement" (Acts 4:36). Some people seem to just come into the world being good encouragers. One of my grandsons is like that. He is always telling other kids what a good job they did or how well they played a game. He is an encourager and a joy to be around. With an encouraging personality, Barnabas would probably have been popular with many people. Word may have spread regarding the donation of land by Barnabas and may have laid the foundation for his reputation as a good man.

At this time, Saul was beginning to make a name for himself in the church as a believer instead of a persecutor, but many of the Christians were still terrified of him. He had hauled people off to jail just for believing in Jesus; he had been right in the middle of the persecution of the saints. The Christians found it hard to believe Saul had made a 180-degree turnaround. They certainly did not want to accept him into the brotherhood. But Barnabas stood up for Saul and persuaded the others to accept him (Acts 9:26-27). This is just the beginning of what we see in Barnabas over and over. He was not afraid to speak out; he boldly proclaimed the truth. He evidently had the power of persuasion or "the gift of gab," for, as on this occasion, the people listened and responded to him. It may also be that the people knew Barnabas's reputation as a good man, full of faith, and they trusted him.

While the church was still young, Stephen was killed by stoning, and the believers, all of whom were Jews, were scattered by the persecution. Some Christians went to Antioch and spread the good news to Jews and then to the Greeks, who also believed. The church in Jerusalem heard about this and decided to send a man to find out exactly what was going on. They chose Barnabas to go and encourage the people to "continue with the Lord" (Acts 11:23). These young Christians needed the encouragement of a man like Barnabas.

Barnabas soon saw another door of opportunity being opened when he would be able to teach the Gentiles about Christ. Because this was a new and huge undertaking, he went to seek out Saul to help him (Acts 11:25-26). Together, they taught many people and led them to Jesus.

According to Acts 11:27-30, while Barnabas and Saul were in Antioch, the prophet Agabus foretold a widespread famine that would take place. The disciples saw this as an opportunity to help their brethren. This is the first time we are told of Gentile Christians aiding their Jewish brothers and sisters. They collected money to buy food during a famine in Judea that, according to historians, lasted three to four years. They entrusted the money to Barnabas and Saul, who took it to Jerusalem. Acts 12 relates incidents in the life of Peter. Then the last verse reverts back to Barnabas and Saul after they had taken the benevolent funds to Jerusalem: "And Barnabas and Saul returned from Jerusalem when they had fulfilled their ministry, and they also took with them John whose surname was Mark" (v. 25).

After their return to Antioch, Barnabas and Saul were set apart as some of the first missionaries. How interesting that they were sent out as missionaries from the church in Antioch instead of Jerusalem. They sailed to Cyprus to preach. Why did they go to Cyprus? Because Cyprus was the home of Barnabas, making it a logical choice. It was natural that he would want his friends and neighbors to know of the gospel message. Barnabas was familiar with the area and, hopefully, was well-accepted there.

From this point on, we no longer read of Barnabas and Saul, but Paul and Barnabas. Saul, who was renamed Paul, took the leading role (Acts 13:9). This was also the point where, for whatever reason, John Mark left them (v. 13).

The next chapters in Acts relate how Paul and Barnabas went about fearlessly teaching the truth. They spoke "boldly in the Lord" even when facing opposition (Acts 14:3). Eventually they wound up back in Antioch, where they had started their journey. Unfortunately, Paul and Barnabas had a disagreement one day. They had started to plan a second missionary trip together when they had a difference of opinion.

Now Barnabas was determined to take with them John called Mark. But Paul insisted that they should not take with them the one who had departed from them in Pamphylia, and had not gone with them to the work. Then the contention became so sharp that they parted from one another. And so Barnabas took Mark and sailed to Cyprus; but Paul chose Silas and departed, being commended by the brethren to the grace of God. And he went through Syria and Cilicia, strengthening the churches. (15:37-41)

Both men had strong personalities; they were not afraid to speak their minds. Barnabas wanted to take John Mark, who was Barnabas' cousin (Colossians 4:10), with them on their next excursion, but because John Mark had deserted them previously, Paul wanted to leave him behind. The disagreement was so severe that Barnabas and Paul chose to go their separate ways. Although it must have been painful for them to part from one another, their separation evidently resulted in good with the gospel being strengthened in twice as many places. Barnabas returned to Cyprus while Paul departed for Syria and Cilicia.

The last we read of Barnabas is in Galatians 2:11-16. Paul related this incident to show that Peter did not have authority over him as some of the Jews still claimed. Peter had associated freely with the Gentile Christians until other Jews arrived who might have seen him and disapproved. We are surprised and saddened to read that "even Barnabas" followed Peter's example (v. 13). Paul labeled this action hypocritical and admonished Peter and the others regarding their behavior.

What Lessons Do We Learn From Barnabas?

1. A good reputation will aid your work for the Lord.

The people trusted Barnabas. He was able to teach both Jews and Gentiles because they knew him to be a man of integrity. If your reputation is not respectable, you will have a difficult time teaching people about Jesus.

> *A good name is to be chosen rather than great riches,*
> *loving favor rather than silver and gold. (Proverbs 22:1)*

2. We should speak boldly for the Lord.

God helped Barnabas be bold; He will help us as well. Because we have God on our side, we don't have to be afraid. God has promised us a spirit of power and love and self-control (2 Timothy 1:7).

> *The wicked flee when no one pursues, but*
> *the righteous are bold as a lion. (Proverbs 28:1)*

3. Don't let a disagreement with a fellow Christian keep you from working for the Lord.

We must not let petty disagreements keep us from doing what God wants us to do. Have you ever seen a Christian withdraw from the work of the church over a dispute with another member? Barnabas and Paul "agreed to disagree." Although they did not travel together during their next trip to do mission work, they never stopped in their work for the Lord. And just look at how much they accomplished – the gospel message continued to be preached.

4. Even good people slip sometimes.

Barnabas was a good man, but he was influenced to do wrong by those around him. We must never think we are beyond temptation. We are all sinners who may say or think or do things contrary to God's will. Although Barnabas committed wrong along with Peter, God still loved him. God always loves us even when we take a step in the wrong direction. Christians are not immune to the enticement of sin.

5. We can and should encourage others in the Lord.

Therefore comfort each other and edify one another,
just as you also are doing. (1 Thessalonians 5:11)

The New American Standard Bible uses the words "encourage one another and build up one another" in that verse. Encouragement is such a blessing in our lives. Whether we are going through difficult times with family problems, illness or grief or struggling to stay faithful to God, the encouragement of our brothers and sisters in Christ often gives us the strength we need to make it through the dark times. God wants us to be that source of strength for others, to lend a helping hand or a listening ear, and to encourage those who are facing trials to continue in their walk with the Lord.

Barnabas was a good man who boldly taught the gospel and encouraged others to stay faithful. We should strive to follow his example.

Let's Think About This

1. What differences do you see in the methods of working with others used by Peter, Paul and Barnabas?

2. What are your thoughts concerning the conflict between Paul and Barnabas? Do you think the actions of Barnabas were consistent with his character?

3. Why do you think Barnabas followed Peter's poor example regarding the Gentiles? How does this affect your view of Barnabas? Do we ever outgrow peer pressure?

4. How do your feelings about someone influence your response to their teaching? Is your reputation such that people will believe what you try to teach?

ANANIAS:

Keeping Up Appearances

Acts 5:1-11

Wendell and I went to Asheville, N.C., to celebrate our 45th wedding anniversary. We stayed in a little bit nicer hotel than usual, and like many hotels, they encouraged water conservation, which is a good thing. A sign on the door in the bathroom suggested we use our towels more than once to help conserve water. We had no problem with their asking us to do this. However, we were amused when we came in one afternoon and found that the housekeeping staff had run the dishwasher to clean one glass and one spoon! Seems just a touch hypocritical, doesn't it?

I was talking with a young woman once whose husband was not a Christian. His reason? There are hypocrites in the church. He knew there are people who profess to be Christians but still sin. How sad that this young man and many others like him can't see past the hypocrisy to find their own salvation. Of course, it is also disheartening that there are hypocrites in the church. Dictionary.com defines "hypocrisy" as "a pretense of having a virtuous character, moral or religious beliefs or principles . . . that one does not really possess." It originally comes from the word meaning to play a part or play-acting. Hypocrisy is not a new problem. This lesson concerns one hypocrite in particular, or really two.

We need to understand the setting for the story of Ananias and his wife, Sapphira. The church was young. Thousands of Jews had come to Jerusalem for Pentecost and had heard the gospel message and become

Christians. They prolonged their stay in Jerusalem to receive instruction in the gospel. But where would they sleep? How would they afford food to eat? The Christians living in Jerusalem stepped up to meet the need. They brought money, goods and the proceeds from selling houses and land to give to the apostles to share with those Christians who were lacking (Acts 4:34). This continued until persecution scattered the Christians, who then spread the gospel wherever they went. In Acts 4, we are told of Barnabas, who sold land and brought the money to the apostles, laying "it at the apostles' feet" (v. 37). I picture it like in the old movies when someone would bring a gift to a king and lay it on the floor and then back away while bowing, but that's just me. A lot of Christians contributed money or possessions, but there must have been something special about Barnabas's gift for it to be specifically mentioned. The incident involving Ananias and Sapphira recorded for us in Acts 5 took place right after this.

Ananias sold a piece of property and laid the proceeds at the apostles' feet just as Barnabas had done previously. Ananias and Sapphira, however, had secretly conspired to keep some of the money and say their gift was the total price they had received. It was as if they sold a piece of land for $10,000, donated $5,000, and made everyone believe that was the sale price. Yet they were not required to donate all of the money they had received for their property; their donation was completely voluntary. Ananias could easily have said, "We are giving this amount of money from the profit we made selling our property." That would still have been a good deed; it would still have been generous. Instead, they lied; they tried to make themselves look good. A.T. Robertson, in his book *Some Minor Characters in the New Testament*, explains:

> It is clear that the hearty praise given by the church to Joseph
> Barnabas excited Ananias and Sapphira to follow his example. ...
> They wanted all the credit and applause that had been bestowed upon
> Barnabas without the deprivation of absolutely all this property.[1]

With the help of the Holy Spirit, Peter immediately knew what had happened. Ananias stood there expecting praise, but instead, Peter lashed out at him. Peter pointed out that Ananias and Sapphira did not have to sell the land; it was completely their own decision. And once they sold it, they did not have to give all of the money to the apostles. In fact, they did not have to give any of it. Their sin was not in withholding part of the money, but in lying about it. Peter says, "Why have you conceived this thing in your heart?" (Acts 5:4). What made you even think of such a terrible thing, Ananias? The sinful action of his brother in Christ must have broken Peter's heart.

Ananias keeled over dead. The physical cause of death is not clear. It's not difficult for us to imagine that the shock of Peter's words could have caused a heart attack. On the other hand, it could have been solely a judgment from God without any physical cause. The punishment certainly came from God either way.

The immediate burial seems hasty to us, but in the hot climate of Palestine, dead bodies decayed rapidly, so it was common to bury on the same day as the death and usually within 24 hours after death.[2] The younger men, not the apostles, acted as pallbearers; they wrapped the body of Ananias in cloth, as custom dictated, and carried him out, probably outside the city limits, and buried him. Depending upon a person's economic and social status, burial would either have been in a shallow grave covered with stones or in a cave or tomb hewn out of stone. Somehow I doubt Ananias had the honor of being buried in a tomb of stone.

About three hours later, Sapphira arrived; she was completely unaware of what had taken place. This also seems strange to us that they buried her husband without even telling her. We can only assume it was due to the circumstances surrounding his death.

Our courts today might call what happened next "entrapment." Without admitting he already knew the answer to his question, Peter asked Sapphira, "How much money did you get for your field?" Sapphira answered the way her husband had. Peter's query had been simple. This was black or white, yes or no. There was no gray area. Sapphira was given the opportunity to tell the truth, but she persisted in the lie.

In that instant, she received a double shock: her husband was dead, and she was about to be. She, too, fell down, died and was buried. The men who had buried her husband were at the door, and now they would take her body out as well.

"So great fear came upon all the church and upon all who heard these things" (Acts 5:11). Word must have spread like wildfire regarding the two deaths. The believers were filled with fear. Think about how this would have affected the church. They certainly would have learned "God is not mocked" as we read in Galatians 6:7. *The Zondervan King James Version Commentary* explains:

> *If no dire consequences had followed this act of sin, the results among the believers would have been serious when the deceit became known. Not only would dishonesty have appeared profitable, but the conclusion that the Spirit could be deceived would have followed. It was important to set the course properly at the outset in order to leave no doubt that God will not tolerate such hypocrisy and deceit.*[3]

What Lessons Do We Learn From Ananias?

1. Hypocrisy is a sin.

Jesus saved some of His harshest words for the scribes and Pharisees who were hypocrites. These men acted "holier than thou" when, in fact, they were not even holy to begin with. Nancy Eichman in her book *Seasoning Your Words* writes that they had a "say-one-thing-and-do-another" lifestyle and religion.[4] They masqueraded as righteous spiritual leaders, but their actions proved otherwise. The so-called seven woes that Jesus directed toward these hypocrites are in Matthew 23. The scribes and Pharisees tithed the mint and anise and cummin but neglected the weightier matters of justice and mercy and faith; they cleansed the outside of the cup, but inside it was full of sin; they built tombs to honor the prophets, but were guilty of shedding righteous blood. My favorite picture is the whitewashed tombs filled with dead men's bones, which vividly portrays for us the duplicity of hypocrisy.

> *Woe to you, scribes and Pharisees, hypocrites! For you are like whitewashed tombs which indeed appear beautiful outwardly, but inside are full of dead men's bones and all uncleanness. Even so you also outwardly appear righteous to men, but inside you are full of hypocrisy and lawlessness. (Matthew 23:27-28)*

By consulting other versions, it's clear to see, no matter how it's translated, Jesus took hypocrisy seriously: "How terrible for you" (NCV); "It will be bad for you" (ERV); "What sorrow awaits you" (NLT). Jesus left no doubt that hypocrisy is a sin. As Ananias tried to show his love for others by contributing to the common fund, he forgot to "let love be without hypocrisy" (Romans 12:9).

2. God knows our thoughts and actions.

God the Creator knows our innermost thoughts and secrets. Nothing can be hidden from Him.

If we had forgotten the name of our God, or stretched out our hands to a foreign god, would not God search this out? For He knows the secrets of the heart. (Psalm 44:20-21)

Ananias foolishly thought he could get away with his deception, but God was aware of the thoughts of his heart as well as his actions. He should have heeded the warning of Jesus in Luke 12.

In the meantime, when an innumerable multitude of people had gathered together, so that they trampled one another, He began to say to His disciples first of all, "Beware of the leaven of the Pharisees, which is hypocrisy. For there is nothing covered that will not be revealed, nor hidden that will not be known." (Luke 12:1-2)

3. God will punish the wicked.

If we believe the Bible when we are told God will reward us with heaven, we must also believe when we are told God will punish the wicked. Many people seem to believe that God loves us so much He could never punish us for our sins. God does love us, but He has repeatedly said we must obey Him or face His punishment.

Since it is a righteous thing with God to repay with tribulation those who trouble you, and to give you who are troubled rest with us when the LORD Jesus is revealed from heaven with His mighty angels, in flaming fire taking vengeance on those who do not know God, and on those who do not obey the gospel of our LORD Jesus Christ. These shall be punished

*with everlasting destruction from the presence of the LORD and from
the glory of His power, when He comes, in that Day, to be glorified in
His saints and to be admired among all those who believe, because our
testimony among you was believed. (2 Thessalonians 1:6-10)*

4. Punishment of the sinner is decisive and divine.

Herbert Lockyer in his book *All the Men of the Bible* said the punishment
of Ananias (and Sapphira) was (1) prompt, followed sin immediately;
(2) decisive; (3) conspicuous, before many witnesses; and (4) divine, not
an act of Peter but of God.[5]

The punishment of the sinner today may not always be so prompt and
may not be so conspicuous, but it will be just as decisive and certainly
will come from God.

*Now Enoch, the seventh from Adam, prophesied about these
men also, saying, "Behold, the LORD comes with ten thousands
of His saints, to execute judgment on all, to convict all who are
ungodly among them of all their ungodly deeds which they have
committed in an ungodly way, and of all the harsh things which
ungodly sinners have spoken against Him." (Jude 14-15)*

In 2011, Senator John Ensign of Nevada, once considered a rising star
in the Republican party, admitted to having an affair with a member
of his staff and announced he would not be seeking reelection. Ensign
told his constituents: "There are consequences to sin."[6] Like Ananias,
Senator Ensign learned a valuable lesson. We need to be sure we realize
that sin always has dreadful consequences.

Let's Think About This

1. What sin(s) did Ananias commit? What could he have done instead?

2. Do you think we would behave differently if our punishment were
   as prompt as Ananias's?

3. Why do you think his punishment was death with no chance of repentance? Can you name others in the Bible who shared a similar fate?

4. What effect might it have had on the church had Peter not known about the deceit?

5. Some people say, "Well, I may have done something wrong, but at least I am not hypocritical about it." Is there a problem with this reasoning?

AQUILA:

Tentmaker, Teacher and Host

Acts 18:1-4, 18-26; Romans 16:3-5; 1 Corinthians 16:19; 2 Timothy 4:19

Many years ago when I was a young, inexperienced minister's wife, we invited the pulpit minister, his family and the well-known visiting preacher, who was there for our gospel meeting, to come to dinner one night. I worked all day cleaning the house. I set the table with my good china and silver; I even ironed my linen napkins. I prepared the best meal I knew how to cook. One of my always-turns-out-right dishes was candied sweet potatoes. I had them timed so they would be hot just as everyone arrived. I waited until just before we were ready to eat to put the miniature marshmallows on top and then slipped them back into the oven to brown. When they were perfect, I carefully took them out of the oven and promptly dropped them on the floor. Potatoes flew everywhere! I did the only thing I could do: I cried.

Fortunately some people are truly blessed with the gift of hospitality. A man who shared his home with a houseguest for well over a year certainly qualifies as being a good host. His name is Aquila, but we can't study Aquila without studying Priscilla as they are always mentioned as a team.

In the beginning of Acts 18, we read that Aquila and Priscilla were Jews living in Corinth. They recently had packed up and moved to Corinth from Rome because Emperor Claudius issued a decree banishing all Jews from Rome (v. 2). Paul traveled to Corinth and became acquainted with them. They shared a common occupation in tentmaking.

Paul stayed and worked with Aquila and Priscilla and was a "part-time" preacher on weekends. Each Sabbath he would speak in the synagogues where the people gathered, teaching about Jesus to both Jews and Greeks.

Because no mention is made of a conversion, Aquila and Priscilla likely were already Christians before Paul arrived, although we are not told when they obeyed the gospel. They could have been converted in Rome or possibly while Paul was staying with them in Corinth. Paul lodged with them between one and a half to two years (Acts 18:11). That's a long time for a houseguest; Aquila and Priscilla certainly must have been hospitable people.

The next time Aquila and Priscilla moved, it was to Ephesus, a leading commercial city of the area (Acts 18:18-19). They traveled some with Paul but stayed at Ephesus while he continued on his journeys. Do you notice anything odd about this passage? Before, the Scriptures read "Aquila and Priscilla," but in this instance and most of the others where they are named, it is "Priscilla and Aquila." What can we deduce from this? Maybe Priscilla was the stronger personality of the two, or she may have had a higher social position. When we first learned of Saul, before his name was changed to Paul, we read "Barnabas and Saul" (Acts 11:30) over and over, but as Paul gained recognition, it became "Paul and Barnabas" (13:43).

While in Ephesus, Aquila and Priscilla went to hear a visiting preacher. Apollos spoke at the synagogue; he knew some about Jesus and was eloquent in teaching others, but he knew only the baptism of John. Basically, he was preaching a baptism of repentance but not in the name of Jesus as the Savior (Acts 18:24-25). When Aquila and Priscilla heard him, they took him aside to teach him more fully (v. 26).

They didn't embarrass him publicly by proclaiming he was in error but took him to a private place and spoke the truth in love. Knowing the role of women in Bible times, we might suppose that Priscilla would have stayed in the back room fixing snacks for the men, but it seems she was an active participant in the instruction of Apollos. Because of their teaching of Apollos, he was able to go out and teach others the correct gospel of Jesus Christ (Acts 18:27-28).

In Romans 16:3-5, we learn three more details about Aquila and Priscilla: (1) They moved back to Rome. Probably two to three years had passed since Paul left them in Ephesus, which would have been ample time for them to move again. (2) At some point their lives had been in danger because of their work with Paul. We are not given any details, but evidently the Christians at that time were aware of this incident. (3) We learn the church met in their house. The brethren obviously did not have fancy air-conditioned church buildings such as many of us enjoy today. This hospitable couple opened their home to their fellow Christians to gather for worship.

First Corinthians is a letter Paul wrote while in Ephesus to the church in Corinth. Aquila and Priscilla had packed up the U-Haul and moved once again; this time back to Ephesus. As Paul ended his letter, he sent greetings from Aquila and Priscilla. As previously, the church met in their home (1 Corinthians 16:19).

The last mention in the Scriptures of Aquila and Priscilla is in 2 Timothy 4:19 when Paul sent his personal greetings to them during his imprisonment in Rome.

What Lessons Do We Learn From Aquila?

1. Christians should be hospitable.

Nelson's Illustrated Bible Dictionary defines hospitality as "the practice of entertaining strangers graciously."[1] The Scriptures mention many examples of people who practiced hospitality, such as Abraham (Genesis 18:1-8), the Shunammite woman (2 Kings 4:8-10), Martha (Luke 10:38), and Lydia (Acts 16:14-15).

Hospitality in the Bible did not mean having a party and inviting your friends as we might think of it today. In Bible times, when people traveled from village to village, lodging was not always available. Certainly the early missionaries needed accommodations as they went about teaching. Hospitality was the answer as people opened their homes to strangers, offering them food and drink and a place to rest. What a wonderful display of the love of Christ! As Christians in a busy world, it seems we tend to disregard this marvelous Christian trait. If we are not diligent, we may fail to take advantage of the wonderful opportunities to open our homes to people who need to see Christ living in us.

Be hospitable to one another without grumbling. (1 Peter 4:9)

2. You can work with your spouse to serve the Lord.

Some of us are married; some are widowed; some are divorced; some are single. Many of us have husbands who are active in the work of the church, but some have husbands who are not Christians. Think about how your marital status affects your service to God. If your husband is a faithful Christian, you may be able to work together for the Lord. You can make visits, conduct Bible studies, or deliver meals together. What a joy to share your faith with a spouse!

If you are married to a non-Christian, you may have to select the good works you participate in very carefully. Our marriages will not benefit if we spend all our time helping others but neglect our husbands. I had a friend who had a gift for cooking. She cooked for seemingly everyone who needed food, but her husband felt like others got more attention than he did and became resentful. Certainly we want to continue serving God with the talents He has given us, but we must be sure our actions do not negatively affect our marriages.

3. We should reach out in love to those who need to hear the truth.

When Aquila and Priscilla realized Apollos needed further teaching regarding the gospel, they willingly took him aside and studied with him. They might have said, "He is such a good teacher and is so knowledgeable. How can we teach him?" Another excuse might have been a lack of time. After all, they had all those tents to finish. They might have convinced themselves that because Apollos would not listen to them anyway there was no need to bother trying. In the end, Aquila and Priscilla did not let fear, intimidation or lack of time keep them from helping Apollos come to a fuller understanding of the truth. Jack Exum, in his book *Questions You Have Asked About Soul Winning*, writes, "Keep in mind that Christ did not send us forth under a commission to convert, change, and coerce – but to TEACH, TEACH, TEACH." [2]

If you don't know how to approach someone about Bible study, ask

God to help you. You might want to say something as simple as "I have been thinking a lot about you lately, and I just wondered if you would like to study the Bible with me." If we are going to turn the world upside down for Christ, we must be willing to follow the examples of Aquila and Priscilla as we teach others the gospel message.

4. Serving the Lord should come first.

Having a houseguest for over a year was probably not without its problems. Did Paul throw his dirty robe on the floor or forget to pick up his knives and awls? Having the church meet in their home might have meant extra cleaning or cooking for Priscilla. Surely moving with Paul from city to city had its own challenges. Through it all, Aquila and Priscilla served the Lord. They chose to spend their lives in service to God; we should also make serving God a priority in our daily lives.

In order to be the kind of Christian women God wants us to be, we need to look at the examples of people like Aquila and Priscilla. They worked together to be hospitable; they taught the truth; they served God.

Let's Think About This

1. Are we known as hospitable people? Why, or why not? What keeps you from practicing hospitality?

2. What does it say about Aquila and Priscilla that they were ready to move to Ephesus with Paul?

3. Do you think Priscilla taught Apollos alongside Aquila?

4. Have you or someone you know had worship services in your home? What were the circumstances?

5. How does your marital status affect your service to God?

EUTYCHUS:

A Too-Comfortable Window Seat

Acts 20:7-12

Worship services, what we commonly refer to as "church," are times when many people gather to honor God. As in any gathering, unusual and sometimes embarrassing events take place. My husband, Wendell, was preaching once on the subject "Ye are the light of the world," and a storm knocked the lights out twice during his sermon. Another time he banged his Bible down to make a point, and all his notes gently fluttered to the floor. One brother in the little country congregation where Wendell used to preach was quite elderly and on multiple medications; as a result, he slept through most services. On one occasion brother Robert made sure everybody else was awake by snoring so loudly. At another congregation where we served, a father was taking his little boy out for misbehaving when his son pleaded, "Help. Help. Won't somebody help the boy?" Then there was the man who dozed off just as the Lord's Supper was being served. His wife elbowed him to wake him up, and he loudly hollered, "What?" Embarrassing moments happen – even during worship.

One man was called by Dr. Alexander Whyte "the father of all such as fall asleep under sermons."[1] He is remembered for only one thing – falling asleep in church. His name was Eutychus; we read about him in Acts 20:7-12.

As we read about this scary episode, the first thing we need to note is that it was written by someone who was present on this occasion. The New American Standard Bible reads, "We were gathered together" (Acts 20:7). Luke, the physician, is the accepted writer of Acts and was a companion of Paul. It makes sense that he was in attendance at this worship service and witnessed everything firsthand.

Paul was one of the greatest preachers at that time; he traveled around preaching the gospel. He had been in Troas one week and was getting ready to leave, but he stayed over to worship with the saints on Sunday before departing. How I wish all Christians would plan their traveling around church services! The Christians met on Sunday to partake of the Lord's Supper, and although that was their primary reason for meeting, their time together also included preaching. To get to hear Paul speak was a big deal – like our hearing Marshall Keeble or Jim Bill McInteer or Willard Collins.

The question is, when did their Sunday start? It depends on whether they measured days from midnight to midnight like the Romans or from sundown to sundown like the ancient Jews. If they went by Roman time, the church probably met on Sunday evening because Sunday was not a holiday during which people were free from daily employment. Some of the believers were probably slaves and were unable to come to the assembly until their work was done, so they had what we would call an evening service. If they followed Jewish time, they began their day at sunset, so Sunday began on what we would call Saturday evening. Either way, this meeting probably began in the evening. Paul preached until midnight, and then the Lord's Supper was observed in the wee hours of the morning. The believers met in an upper room because they had no church buildings in which to gather. This room may have been in the private home of one of the believers.

"Many lamps" were in the room (Acts 20:8). The lamps were probably small oil lamps, perhaps small enough to fit in your hand, and they gave off a nice, soft, flickering glow. They may have produced smoke, getting into people's eyes and making them want to close their eyes against it. The lamps also may have contributed to making the temperature in the room very warm.

One of the young men present at this meeting was Eutychus. Eutychus was a common slave name.[2] It's possible he was a slave who had worked all day and was tired, although we are not told such details. His name means "happy or fortunate," which proved to be true.[3] We know Eutychus took a seat in a window. Glass was not in common use at this time; the window was probably just an opening in the wall to let in light and air. The room may have been hot and overcrowded with people crammed in everywhere wanting to hear Paul. Eutychus was so sleepy, and Paul kept preaching and preaching. Adam Clarke, in his commentary, reasons that Paul probably spoke at least six hours![4] Finally Eutychus couldn't hold his eyes open any longer; he fell asleep and fell out the window (Acts 20:9). The tense of the Greek verb indicates he was gradually overcome, not suddenly. Perhaps he really tried to stay awake. The conclusion of Matthew Henry in his 1706 commentary is interesting: "If he could have been content to sit on the floor, he had been safe. Boys that love to climb, or otherwise endanger themselves, to the grief of their parents, consider not how much it is also an offence to God."[5] I really don't know that we can blame Eutychus because he sat in the window instead of on the floor!

How old do you think Eutychus was? Some Bible scholars believe he was a youth, probably from 8 to 14 years of age, while others teach that the original word in Acts 20:9 could indicate a young man from age 24 to age 40.[6]

Eutychus fell from the third story. We do not often think about buildings in Bible times as having three floors, but they evidently did. This window would have been over the street or over the interior court, but regardless of where he fell, the fall killed him. Some people believe he broke his neck, but the Scriptures don't tell us. One of my sons was 18 months old when he managed to slip through the railing of a deck and fell 12 feet to the ground below. When we heard his cry, we ran to look over the railing first and then rushed down the stairs to see if he was hurt. Fortunately, he did not sustain any serious injuries. I can picture the people, perhaps after seeing Eutychus fall or hearing his scream, run over to look out the window and then hurry down the stairs to check on him. Imagine their dismay when they found him dead. Remember, this is Dr. Luke telling us this, and he evidently believed Eutychus was dead and not just asleep. As a physician, he would have known the difference.

Paul followed the crowd outside. When he saw Eutychus, Paul kneeled down, hugged him to himself, and said, "Do not trouble yourselves, for his life is in him" (Acts 20:10). Life was restored to the young man. Thankfully, as one writer says, "God has mercy on church snoozers."[7] After performing this miracle, Paul calmly went back to preaching. I suspect Eutychus stayed awake for that sermon.

Paul's action in restoring life to Eutychus reminds us of Elijah and Elisha. Elijah brought life back to the widow's son while Elisha returned the Shunammite woman's son to her.

> *And he stretched himself out on the child three times,*
> *and cried out to the LORD and said, "O LORD my God, I pray,*
> *let this child's soul come back to him." (1 Kings 17:21)*

> *And he went up and lay on the child, and put his mouth*
> *on his mouth, his eyes on his eyes, and his hands on his hands;*
> *and he stretched himself out on the child, and the flesh of the*
> *child became warm. (2 Kings 4:34)*

Other than the resurrection of Christ and of those whose lives were restored following His crucifixion, the raising of Eutychus is the last of eight resurrections described for us in the Bible.

The people brought the boy in alive, and they were greatly comforted. It was a cause for great rejoicing among them. Paul would leave them, but what an encouragement to their faith to have witnessed this miracle right before he left.

The only time Eutychus got his name in Scripture was when he died while sleeping during worship. The writer of Acts included this incident for all the world to read. Charles Swindoll writes: "If the same thing happened to sleepers today, every church would have to build a morgue in the basement. ... If you sit in the balcony and get sleepy, watch out! Eutychus 'being dead, yet speaketh.'"[8]

Consider the reasons we may sleep during worship even when we know we ought to stay awake.[9]

1. Physical reasons. We have nice, padded pews and comfortable heating or air conditioning; everything works together to make us feel relaxed and at ease. It's just too easy to drift off to sleep. Remember all those nice little flickering lamps giving off a soft glow that Eutychus had to contend with? And it was late! Paul had been preaching on and on. Could we have stayed awake any better than Eutychus?

2. Habit. Sleeping during worship may be a habit; it is a bad habit, but a habit nonetheless. When we were children, we got comfy on the pew and took a nap, and our parents were pleased. As adults, we sit up straight, but our eyes still close.

3. Personal issues. A lack of sufficient sleep on Saturday night can have dire results on Sunday morning. We stay out late and then don't understand why we cannot stay awake during worship. Perhaps we've been on the go all week without sufficient rest, and this is the first time we have been still. Or we may be on medication like brother Robert was or have a medical condition that makes it difficult to stay awake.

4. Apathy. Some people are simply not interested in the worship service. They do not care what is being said; they are not paying close attention. They are not personally involved in the worship of God. If your mind wanders, if you do not focus on God, it is easy to succumb to the enticing release of sleep.

5. An uninteresting messenger. Sadly, some preachers are boring – not due to the gospel message they bring but because they ramble or mumble or speak too slow or too fast. Some ministers use a monotonous tone that is somewhat sing-song and lulls us into a light sleep.

To avoid going to sleep as Eutychus did, it is helpful to have a building conducive to worship, not too hot and not too cold; a speaker delivering the message clearly and concisely; and a worshiper prepared to worship, rested in mind and body, alert and interested in the message.

What Lessons Do We Learn From Eutychus?

1. We should prepare ourselves to worship God.

Before the Israelites gathered at the base of Mount Sinai for God's appearance, they were instructed to consecrate themselves and wash their clothes.

Then the LORD said to Moses, "Go to the people and consecrate them today and tomorrow, and let them wash their clothes. And let them be ready for the third day. For on the third day the LORD will come down upon Mount Sinai in the sight of all the people." (Exodus 19:10-11)

Meeting God at the foot of the mountain was an important occasion, and they needed to be prepared spiritually, mentally and physically. Preparation for worship is just as important today. Our thoughts should be centered on God as we approach worship. We need to have the right frame of mind. Plenty of rest on Saturday night should be a priority. We should dress appropriately so as not to be too hot or too cold.

2. We should be wholly involved in worship to God.

After the Babylonian captivity, Ezra the priest led a group of Jews back to Jerusalem to rebuild the city. With Nehemiah's help, they were finally able to finish the work. All the people then gathered together and asked Ezra to read to them from the book of the Law of Moses.

Then he read from it in the open square that was in front of the Water gate from morning until midday, before the men and women and those who could understand; and the ears of all the people were attentive to the Book of the Law. (Nehemiah 8:3)

Worship is a privilege, and we should be fully involved and attentive. We should listen and focus on what's being said and done; we should participate in singing and prayer and study. Our minds should be centered on God and His Son.

3. We should believe in the great power of God.

By the power of God, Paul restored life to Eutychus. Our God is great and mighty; He is deserving of our worship and praise. When we think of all the blessings God has so richly bestowed on us, we will want to worship and praise Him.

All nations whom You have made shall come and worship before You, O LORD, and shall glorify Your name. For You are great, and do wondrous things; You alone are God. (Psalm 86:9-10)

Let's Think About This

1. What preparations do you make to be ready to worship God?

2. If sleepiness during worship is a problem, what are some suggestions to help us stay awake?

3. What are some suggestions to help children learn to behave during worship?

4. How old should children be when they quit sleeping in worship?

5. How might the restoration of life to Eutychus have affected the church in Troas?

6. List reasons God deserves our worship.

10

PHILIP, ONE OF THE TWELVE:

The Left-Brained Man

John 1:40-46; 6:1-14; 12:20-22; 14:1-10; Acts 1:13

Experimentation has shown that the two sides, or hemispheres, of the brain are responsible for two different "modes" of thinking – labeled left-brain and right-brain. Left-brained people are logical, rational, analytical, objective and detail-oriented. Right-brained people are creative, imaginative, intuitive, subjective and look at the big picture. I have always thought I was a left-brained person because I see myself as very organized and logical. When I started researching the brain on the Internet, it listed all kinds of tests to determine whether you are left-brained or right-brained. I took one of the tests and was amazed when it said I was right in the middle, both left-brained and right-brained. I knew that couldn't be correct so I took a completely different test. This test gave a number for each side of the brain, and whichever number was higher indicated which side dominated. On this test I scored 16 on the left side and 16 on the right side. I am obviously not as logical as I thought.

One man in the Scriptures seems left-brained to me. He is Philip, one of the 12 apostles. Later we will study a second Philip, one of the seven deacons. We will learn which one did what. They were both faithful disciples, Christians in the early church, and evangelistic. We never read of Philip the apostle after Pentecost nor of Philip the deacon before Pentecost. It is interesting to note that Philip is a Greek name although they were both Jews.

Philip is named in the lists of apostles in Matthew, Mark and Luke, and his name is always fifth, but we are unsure of any significance in that. *Smith's Bible Dictionary* did point out he was the first in the second group of four, implying they were listed in order of importance. His name means "lover of horses."[1] Philip was from Bethsaida, a small fishing village on the west shore of the Sea of Galilee that was also the home of Andrew and Peter.

Andrew, Peter and Philip all probably journeyed to Bethany to hear the teaching of John the Baptist. John the Baptist, of course, pointed them to Jesus. In the first recorded instance of Jesus calling a disciple, Jesus said to Philip, "Follow Me" (John 1:43). Earlier Andrew had told Peter about Jesus; now Philip found Nathanael and told him about Jesus. When Nathanael balked at the thought of Jesus being the Messiah, Philip didn't argue with him or walk away, but invited him to see for himself (vv. 45-46). He used a very simple and direct approach. The *Encyclopedia of the Bible* says this: "He is portrayed as a naive, rather shy, but sober-minded person. Philip was timid and retiring; yet he informed Nathanael that he had discovered the Messiah foretold in the Old Testament."[2] If we could just follow that example of Philip, how much increase would we see in the Lord's followers!

We see Philip next at the familiar miracle when Jesus fed over 5,000 people (John 6:1-14). Great crowds of people followed Jesus. Harold Willmington in *Willmington's Bible Handbook* estimates that Jesus miraculously fed as many as 20,000 people including all the women and children.[3] Jesus saw these thousands of people, knew they were hungry, and asked Philip, "Where shall we buy bread, that these may eat?" (v. 5). From Luke's account, we learn that the location of this miracle was close to Bethsaida (Luke 9:10-11). Who better than Philip, who was from that area, to know where to acquire food? Scripture says Jesus asked Philip in order to test him. Jesus already knew what He was going to do to solve the problem. Herbert Lockyer in *All the Men of the Bible* writes, "Philip was singled out for a test of his faith, and for a great opportunity, which he lost, and with it lost a blessing."[4]

Philip's actions were those of a left-brained person; he did the logical thing. He quickly calculated how many people there were times how much they would eat and figured out how much it would cost. Do you think this shows a lack of faith on his part? Does it show a lack of understanding or imagination? Moses had done the same thing. Early in their wanderings in the desert, when the people complained that they wanted meat to eat in addition to the manna, God told them, "Okay, I will give you meat. I will give you so much meat that you will eat it every day for a month and be sick of it" (cf. Numbers 11:18-20). Moses immediately started adding up how many flocks and herds would have to be slaughtered to feed over 600,000 people (vv. 21-23) This was soon after Moses had watched God send the 10 plagues to Egypt, but it didn't occur to him that God could send this much meat to feed the Israelites.

In light of this, maybe it wasn't so strange that Philip didn't understand how Christ could feed a multitude. In Philip's defense, this was before the miraculous feeding of the 4,000, and a large percentage of the miracles that had been done up to this time were of healing. Maybe he had trouble translating that into something as material as food. It just didn't occur to him to think outside the box. He analyzed the problem and was unable to see an answer.

During the time of Jesus' final Passover in Jerusalem, great multitudes had come for the feast, including some Greeks. They had heard about Jesus and wanted to meet Him; they sought out Philip and told him of their desire (John 12:20-21). Why Philip? Remember Philip was a Greek name; it is possible he was born among the Greeks and spoke the same language, or Philip may have been originally from the same area as these men. The *International Standard Bible Encyclopedia* says about Philip that "he himself possessed an inquirer's spirit and could therefore sympathize with their doubts and difficulties."[5]

We are not told why Philip did not go directly to Jesus; instead, he told Andrew of the Greeks' desire, and together they went to tell Jesus of their request to see Him (John 12:22). Perhaps Philip doubted whether Jesus would want to speak with these Greek men and wanted to seek Andrew's opinion. Jesus then spoke of His coming death, probably within the Greeks' hearing (vv. 23-32).

After Jesus ate the Passover feast with His disciples, He continued to prepare them for His coming death. Jesus comforted them with the beautiful words we read in John 14:

> *Let not your heart be troubled; you believe in God, believe also*
> *in Me. In My Father's house are many mansions; if it were not so,*
> *I would have told you. I go to prepare a place for you. And if I go*
> *and prepare a place for you, I will come again and receive you to*
> *Myself; that where I am, there you may be also. And where I go*
> *you know, and the way you know. (vv. 1-4)*

Thomas expressed the confusion that many of the disciples probably felt when he replied that they did not know where Jesus was going and did not know the way (John 14:5). Jesus explained that the only path to the Father is through His Son.

> *Jesus said to him, "I am the way, the truth, and the life.*
> *No one comes to the Father except through Me. If you had*
> *known Me, you would have known My Father also; and*
> *from now on you know Him and have seen Him." (vv. 6-7)*

Philip still did not comprehend and replied, "Lord, show us the Father, and it is sufficient for us" (John 14:8). Perhaps he was asking for a literal viewing of God as when Moses said to God, "Please, show me Your glory" (Exodus 33:18). Or maybe Philip was just asking for more understanding. Again, Philip seems to be a practical, down-to-earth, logical kind of fellow in this instance. He doesn't seem to be imaginative but a person who used just the left side of his brain in a thoughtful kind of way. Jesus offered Philip a very direct answer:

> *Have I been with you so long, and yet you have not known Me, Philip?*
> *He who has seen Me has seen the Father; so how can you say, "Show*
> *us the Father"? Do you not believe that I am in the Father, and the*
> *Father in Me? The words that I speak to you I do not speak on My own*
> *authority; but the Father who dwells in Me does the works. Believe*
> *Me that I am in the Father and the Father in Me, or else believe Me for*
> *the sake of the works themselves. (John 14:9-11)*

When we last read of Philip the apostle by name, he was right where he was supposed to be – in Jerusalem with the other followers awaiting the Holy Spirit after the death and resurrection of Christ (Acts 1:13). These are among the few details we are given about the life of Philip the apostle; however, we know he was commended when Jesus chose him to be one of His special messengers to the world. Philip sought out the truth and spent his life working for Jesus.

What Lessons Do We Learn From Philip, One of the Twelve?

1. We can all tell others about Jesus.

Oh, give thanks to the LORD, for He is good! For His mercy endures forever. Let the redeemed of the LORD say so, whom He has redeemed from the hand of the enemy. (Psalm 107:1-2)

The Bible in Basic English translates Psalm 107:1-2 in these words: "Let those whose cause the Lord has taken up say so, his people whom he has taken out of the hands of their haters." The New Living Translation reads: "Has the LORD redeemed you? Then speak out!" It doesn't matter whether we are logical and detached or emotional and outgoing; we can speak up for the cause of Christ because we have been redeemed. Once Philip believed, he immediately began telling others about the Savior. He told Nathanael about Jesus; he led the Greeks to Jesus. Every day we meet people who need to know Jesus as their Savior. Do we lead them to Him?

2. We must never underestimate the power of God.

Philip could not see any way Jesus could feed well over 5,000 people; there just wasn't that much food or money available. He was looking for an earthly answer, but he did not take into account the power of God. The disciples did the same thing when a storm arose and threatened their safety in a boat. They were frightened and could not see a way out (Matthew 8:23-27). In both instances, Jesus provided a miraculous solution to their problems. Do we look for answers in the wrong places instead of trusting in the amazing power of God? Sometimes we have a problem, and we can't see any remedy. But are we looking at it only from a worldly point of view? We need to adjust our vision to see things with a spiritual eye, never underestimating the power of God (cf. Matthew 19:26).

3. We must be approachable so people will come to us with their questions about Jesus.

The Greeks evidently felt comfortable talking to Philip and knew he could help them with their desire to know more about Jesus. Do people see our relationship with Jesus? Does our attitude invite questions about our faith, or does it turn people away?

But sanctify the LORD God in your hearts, and always be ready to give a defense to everyone who asks you a reason for the hope that is in you, with meekness and fear. (1 Peter 3:15)

4. We should look closely at the Son so we can see the Father.

If we want to know God, we must be familiar with His Son, "the express image of His person" (Hebrews 1:3). We achieve that the same way Philip did – by spending time with Him. We are not blessed to be face-to-face with Jesus on this earth as Philip was, but we can know Him through the Scriptures. Through our study of the Bible, we are blessed to know both the Father and the Son.

He has delivered us from the power of darkness and conveyed us into the kingdom of the Son of His love, in whom we have redemption through His blood, the forgiveness of sins. He is the image of the invisible God, the firstborn over all creation. (Colossians 1:13-15)

Let's Think About This

1. In what ways could Philip be described as left-brained?

2. Why do you think Jesus tested Philip? Are we ever tested? Why?

3. What do you think Philip learned about Jesus after He miraculously fed the multitude?

4. What can we learn from Philip about talking to our friends about Jesus? Is a direct approach sometimes best?

5. We see God the Father through Jesus the Son. Name traits that we see in both God and Jesus.

PHILIP, ONE OF THE SEVEN:

Answering the Call

Acts 6:1-7; 8:1-17, 26-40; 21:8-9

It was about midnight. I had been asleep over an hour, but I awoke to the sound of a voice in the garage below me. Curious, I made my way downstairs to find out what was going on. I found my husband in the garage – talking to a baby skunk! Wendell had stayed up late studying when he heard a noise in the garage and went to investigate. He saw the poor little skunk, which had gotten trapped in the garage. The skunk was frightened, and Wendell was speaking to him in a gentle voice, trying to keep him calm. The problem, of course, was how to get the skunk out of the garage without upsetting him and causing an even bigger problem. Obviously, talking to him was not getting us anywhere. I searched the refrigerator and offered the animal a meal of lettuce and carrots, but the skunk must not have been hungry; he ignored the goodies. Wendell finally placed an open box close to the skunk and used a broom to gently usher him into it. The skunk was given his freedom, and the problem was solved.

Problems confront us every day, and solutions must be found. The first we read of the second Philip, not Philip the apostle, is in the context of a problem in the early church. In Jerusalem, probably a few years after the beginning of the church, Christians were numerous and showed charity to one another with a daily distribution of food (Acts 6:1). There were two groups of believers: the Hebrews (Jews who were born in Palestine and spoke Hebrew or Aramaic) and the Greek-speaking Jews (referred to as Hellenistic Jews). This second group was made up of Jews who were born in another country and spoke the Greek language.[1] The Hellenistic Jews complained that the widows among them were being neglected, something that did not seem fair. It is possible that each group tried to look after the welfare of their own widows without purposefully neglecting the others.

The apostles recognized a problem existed but did not believe they should neglect their duty of preaching to determine how to distribute food and goods. Instead, they determined a better resolution to the situation. The apostles called the church together and instructed them to choose seven good, faithful men to do this job (Acts 6:2-5). The Scriptures do not label them as deacons, but their duties sound comparable to that position. The believers thought this was a good idea, and they picked seven men: Stephen, Philip and five others. All seven men had Greek names. It makes sense they chose men from the Greek-speaking Jews, the same group that believed their widows were being treated unfairly. Stephen, who would soon face martyrdom, and Philip are the only two ever mentioned again in Scripture. The apostles "laid [their] hands on them," the method used in Scripture to induct into office or give a job (v. 6). We know from this incident that Philip was a faithful man who was honest and wise, and he had a good reputation in the early church.

After the martyrdom of Stephen, the plight of the Christians worsened with increasing maltreatment. Persecution became rampant. For merely believing in Christ, people were hauled out of their houses and dragged to jail. The persecution instigated by Saul of Tarsus probably stopped the daily distribution of food with which the deacons were charged. In response to the persecution, Christians escaped to the regions of Judea and Samaria with the exception of the apostles who stayed in Jerusalem. This is the first we read in Acts of the gospel being carried beyond the borders of Jewish territory.[2] Philip was one of those who was "scattered abroad" by the persecution (Acts 8:1-4).

The persecution that was meant to destroy Christians resulted in the beginning of the missionary movement. Don't you just love that the result of the persecution of the church was the expansion of the gospel to other people? Philip, one of the seven, who was "full of the Holy

Spirit and wisdom" (Acts 6:3), became an evangelist as he departed to Samaria and began preaching. One reason we know it was this Philip is because the apostles stayed in Jerusalem, which would have included Philip the apostle. This Philip, the servant and evangelist, preached and performed miracles, and many were baptized. His preaching, accompanied by miracles of healing and the casting out of demons, turned the allegiance of the entire city to Christ (8:5-13).

Does anything surprise you about this passage? How about the fact that they were Samaritans? Remember, Jews did not want anything to do with Samaritans. That's because Samaritans were considered a mixed race that had descended from captive Jews who had intermarried with Gentiles. The Samaritans also practiced a false religion, a mixture of worshiping God and the false gods of the Assyrians. Philip broke through the Jewish anti-Samaritan prejudice and obeyed the command given by Jesus to preach the gospel as a witness in Samaria (Acts 1:8). In fact, Philip was one of the heroic first to admit non-Jewish believers into the fellowship of the church. Prior to this, Samaritans were excluded and even denied the privilege of becoming Jewish proselytes. Philip and not the apostles, surprisingly, took the first step in (1) overcoming Jewish prejudice and (2) expanding the church in accordance with the Lord's command. In this regard, Philip was a forerunner of Paul, the apostle to the Gentiles. Philip's missionary work reveals to us one free from the religious prejudices of the strict Jewish Christian.

Another way we know this Philip was not Philip the apostle is because this Philip could not lay his hands on the Samaritan converts so they could receive the Holy Spirit. Instead, Peter and John had to come down from Jerusalem to perform this duty as that gift came only through the apostles (Acts 8:14-17). The laying on of hands was for the special gift of the Holy Spirit that produced the ability to do miracles, not the Spirit promised with baptism (6:6, 8; 8:6-8).

An angel provided instructions to Philip for his next encounter, which is related for us in Acts 8:26-40. Philip was told to go south to the road that descended from Jerusalem to Gaza, although he was not given specific instructions regarding what awaited him there. He obeyed immediately. Upon arrival, Philip saw a man from Ethiopia, an ancient country south of Egypt, a distance of about 200 miles from Jerusalem.[3]

This man was an important officer in the service of Candace, the queen of the Ethiopians, and had been to Jerusalem to worship. Now he was returning home in a chariot. Because he was from Ethiopia, this man would have been a Gentile. Again, Philip did not let that stop him; Philip was eager to teach him the good news about Jesus.

Scripture tells us the Ethiopian man was a eunuch. Usually the purpose in performing castration on a man was to keep him from being tempted with lustful desires when in contact with the royal women. *Adam Clarke's Commentary* explains any government officer was called a eunuch whether he was castrated or not; thus, we are unsure how this term applied to the Ethiopian.[4]

This man was probably a proselyte, or convert, to the Jewish faith. His long journey to Jerusalem to worship, his study of the Scriptures, and his willingness to be taught all indicate he was a believer in God and was seeking the truth. We are struck by what lengths a true believer will go in an effort to be obedient.

Philip went close to the chariot and heard the man reading aloud. That he was not reading silently seems a little strange to our ears, but this was the traditional manner in antiquity.[5] When Philip simply asked him if he understood what he was reading, the man replied, "How can I, unless someone guides me?" (Acts 8:31).

The passage the Ethiopian was reading was from Isaiah 53:7-8. We can understand that these verses refer to Jesus because we have the benefit of the entirety of the Scriptures, and we have been taught that Jesus was sacrificed "as a lamb to the slaughter" (v. 7). We know John referred to Jesus as "the Lamb of God" (John 1:29). The Ethiopian did not have this knowledge and needed someone to teach him.

Philip taught him the good news about Jesus, the very same good news we have today and with the same results. Philip "preached Jesus to him"; Philip must have taught about the Son of God and His sacrifice for our sins as well as the need for repentance and baptism. When they came to a body of water, the Ethiopian asked if there was anything to prevent him from being baptized (Acts 8:35-36). Philip took the Ethiopian down to the water and immersed him. The Ethiopian rejoiced as he came out of the waters of baptism. Philip the evangelist was taken away by the Spirit to a city called Azotus, his first stop on the way to

Caesarea (vv. 39-40). He continued preaching the good news about Jesus to those who needed to hear.

The last we read of Philip the evangelist is 20 to 25 years later when we find him settled in the town of Caesarea (Acts 21:8-9). We have no doubt that this is Philip the servant and the evangelist, for he is described as one of the seven. Paul, on one of his journeys, stopped in and stayed with the still-faithful Philip and his four daughters, who all possessed the gift of prophetic utterance and who apparently gave themselves to the work of teaching. Perhaps during this visit Luke heard from Philip's own lips the details about his endeavors, which Luke then recorded in Acts.

What Lessons Do We Learn From Philip, One of the Seven?

1. Christians will face persecution.

Stephen was stoned to death for proclaiming his faith in Jesus. What happened to the other Christians? Surely they were in danger as well. Those early Christians in Jerusalem had to leave their homes to escape physical persecution. Others were not so fortunate during the first few hundred years of the church as they faced stoning, being burned to death or crucifixion.

We often think of persecution as a long-dead problem, but in our world, Christians are facing mistreatment and even death because of belief in Jesus Christ. On Oct. 25, 2016, terrorists targeted Christians at a hotel in northeast Kenya, killing 12 and injuring several others. In the same month, 48 Christians were slaughtered in Nigeria; the assailants also burned their houses and destroyed farms. In the United States, Christians are being criticized, humiliated and sued in the courts for standing up for their beliefs and values. We should not be surprised when facing cruelty, oppression and violence as Jesus warned His followers to expect persecution from those in the world just as He was persecuted.

Remember the word that I said to you, "A servant is not greater than his master." If they persecuted Me, they will also persecute you. If they kept My word, they will keep yours also. (John 15:20)

79

2. We must remain faithful in the face of persecution.

The early Christians left their homes, but they did not desert their God. They remained strong in their faith and taught the truth to others. Fear probably gripped them at times, but even when faced with opposition, they stayed true to their God, continuing in the things they had learned as Paul wrote in his letter to Timothy:

> *Yes, and all who desire to live godly in Christ Jesus will suffer persecution. But evil men and impostors will grow worse and worse, deceiving and being deceived. But you must continue in the things which you have learned and been assured of, knowing from whom you have learned them, and that from childhood you have known the Holy Scriptures, which are able to make you wise for salvation through faith which is in Christ Jesus. (2 Timothy 3:12-15)*

3. We can look forward to the reward.

Philip, Stephen, the rest of the seven "deacons," and the other Christians at that time lived faithfully even when facing persecution because they understood the reward that awaits the righteous. We have that same reward promised if we will stay faithful to the end.

> *Blessed are those who are persecuted for righteousness'*
> *sake, for theirs is the kingdom of heaven. (Matthew 5:10)*

We don't know the end of the life story of Philip, but we do know that even in his later years, he continued to be faithful to God. Christianity is not a temporary venture; it is a way of life to the end. Philip teaches us not to be afraid of the judgments and actions of those who don't know Christ but to lovingly share the good news with all people.

Let's Think About This

1. Read the qualifications of deacons in 1 Timothy 3:8-10. From what we know of Philip, did he share these characteristics?

2. Discuss other instances of the laying on of hands in Scripture and its purpose.

3. Do some Christians exhibit prejudice today? How can we overcome our prejudices?

4. Christians are often ridiculed and sometimes persecuted for being intolerant. How should we react to these accusations?

5. How can we show support for Christians who are facing trials for their faith in our own country and around the world?

6. Like the Ethiopian, many people today claim to be religious or spiritual but have no true understanding of the Bible. How can we reach them with the gospel message?

DEMAS:

A Love Affair With the World

Colossians 4:10-14; 2 Timothy 4:9-10; Philemon 24

Alexander Graham Bell is commonly credited as the inventor of the first practical telephone on March 10, 1876. The classic story of his crying out "Mr. Watson, come here – I want to see you!" is a well-known part of American history. Over the next few years, the wooden crank phone was developed; then came the candlestick phone used from the 1890s to the 1940s. From 1905 through 1930, a candlestick phone with a rotary dial was used. Then came the rotary dial phone that, by the 1950s, had evolved into the phones we now see in antique malls. I purchased an iPhone a few months ago. This phone has various applications or apps. One little app shows today's date. Another one takes pictures and even videos. If you touch this spot, it will bring up the weather. Need a map? Touch here. Want to know what the stock market is doing? Just press here. If you need a stopwatch, an alarm or a timer, touch the little clock. And this small device can also make phone calls! I suspect Alexander Graham Bell would have a hard time recognizing this as a telephone.

Communication has changed greatly over the years. The ways we communicate today would seem like magic to people who lived 200-plus years ago. People alive even 50 years ago are astonished at the technology that has become so common today. Imagine how the people in Bible times would marvel at the ease and speed with which we can talk with people around the world. The early gospel preachers had only two methods of communication: they could tell people the good news directly or write their words in letter form. Although Paul was often hindered from preaching to the multitudes face-to-face because of his imprisonments, he was able to write everything down that he wanted to say and send the letters by a messenger. Many times these letters were then circulated among the area congregations. Three of those letters written by Paul, each to a different address, mention a man named Demas.

Demas is relatively unknown to us because so little was written about him. I frequently read the Bible story book to my children titled *Tiny Tots' Bible Reader* written by Jim Bill McInteer. The story of Demas is told in this book, and he is often referred to as "Demas, poor Demas," and that is still how I think of him.

The first we read of Demas is in Paul's letter to the Colossians. The book of Colossians was written from prison in Rome during Paul's first imprisonment when he was under house arrest. He wrote letters and had them delivered to the various recipients. The letter to the church at Colossae begins, as do most of Paul's letters, by saying "Paul, an apostle of Christ Jesus." We usually sign our names at the end of correspondence, but there was a very good reason Paul placed his name at the beginning of the letter instead of the end. Letters were written on a roll of papyrus, leather or parchment and rolled up on a stick. A scroll containing the book of Luke or Acts could have been as long as 35 feet! Even longer books of the Bible would have required more than one scroll.[1] Although these letters of Paul were somewhat shorter, if their recipients wanted to know who wrote them, they wouldn't have wanted to unroll the entire scroll to find the name at the bottom. Thus, the name usually went at the beginning.

The end of this letter to the church at Colossae mentions greetings from people obviously well-known to the Colossians such as Aristarchus, Mark and Luke (Colossians 4:10-14). It would be as if I wrote you a letter and added, "Wendell says hello." One of those referred to in this letter is Demas, and it just mentions that he sent his greetings. While Paul made remarks about most of the others whose names were mentioned, he did not make any personal comment about Demas.

About the same time Paul wrote the letter to the Colossians around

A.D. 62, he wrote a more personal letter to an individual named Philemon. This time Demas was said to be one of Paul's "fellow laborers" (Philemon 24). All we know about him at this point is that he was evidently a Christian working with Paul. Of course, that is saying a good bit because Paul was a prisoner at this time. As far as we know, Demas was not imprisoned, but as a Christian, the threat would surely have been hanging over his head.

According to Bible scholars, Paul was released from prison, engaged for a few more years in missionary work, and was then arrested and imprisoned a second time in Rome. From this imprisonment, nearing the end of his life, Paul wrote a second letter to his fellow worker Timothy. News of Demas was also relayed in this letter.

Be diligent to come to me quickly; for Demas has forsaken me, having loved this present world, and has departed for Thessalonica – Crescens for Galatia, Titus for Dalmatia. (2 Timothy 4:9-10)

The Easy-to-Read Version says in plain words, "Demas loved this world too much. That is why he left me." Oh, Demas, poor Demas. Paul was in need of his companions; he was elderly and facing severe trials, perhaps even death. But Demas abandoned Paul to go back to the sinful world.

What about Crescens and Titus? Did they desert Paul as well or were they sent to work for the Lord in other locations? All we are told is that Crescens went to Galatia and Titus to Dalmatia. It is possible that they followed the example of Demas and left Paul or that they were carrying the gospel to the lost in those cities.

What we do know is what Paul said: Demas loved the world too much. Think about the world he loved. He was in Rome, which even at that time was a major metropolis. He saw the magnificent halls of the Caesars, the night life, the riches, people living in grand splendor. In comparison, he was with Paul, an old man in prison. What future would Demas have with Paul? Paul was possibly headed for execution. If Demas was not careful, he might go right along with him. Even if he escaped death, he could foresee trouble and maltreatment. Maybe Demas remembered how Paul had described his life in his earlier letter to Timothy.

But you have carefully followed my doctrine, manner of life, purpose, faith, longsuffering, love, perseverance, persecutions, afflictions, which happened to me at Antioch, at Iconium, at Lystra – what persecutions I endured. And out of them all the LORD delivered me. Yes, and all who desire to live godly in Christ Jesus will suffer persecution. (2 Timothy 3:10-12)

Persecutions! Afflictions! What a dilemma Demas faced – spending his days pursuing money and pleasure or a life filled with persecution. Maybe Demas wondered, "Is being a Christian worth such a sacrifice?" Perhaps he looked at Paul in prison and questioned if he was strong enough to live his life as a Christian. The fear of his own death at the hands of the Romans may have persuaded him to abandon his colleague Paul. Sadly, Demas chose the worldly life. He loved his life and did not want to chance losing it for Christ by staying around Paul. It sounds as though he even forsook Christ. *All the Men of the Bible* by Herbert Lockyer explains, "This man of wavering impulse who surrendered the passion of sacrifice and sank in the swirling waters of the world, is a true reflection of the thought that where our love is, there we finally are."[2] *Matthew Henry's Commentary* states, "Love to this present world is often the cause of apostasy from the truths and ways of Jesus Christ."[3]

In Luke 8 we have the parable of the sower, which Jesus told. As the sower scattered his seed, some of the seed "fell among thorns, and the thorns sprang up with it and choked it" (v. 7). The disciples had trouble understanding the meaning of this parable and asked Jesus to explain.

Now the parable is this: The seed is the word of God. Those by the wayside are the ones who hear; then the devil comes and takes away the word out of their hearts, lest they should believe and be saved. But the ones on the rock are those who, when they hear, receive the word with joy; and these have no root, who believe for a while and in time of temptation fall away. Now the ones that fell among thorns are those who, when they have heard, go out and are choked with cares, riches, and pleasures of life, and bring no fruit to maturity. But the ones that fell on the good ground are those who, having heard the word with a noble and good heart, keep it and bear fruit with patience. (Luke 8:11-15)

Demas was like the seed that fell among thorns. Cares, riches and pleasures of life grew up to stifle his faith and ultimately stopped Demas from bearing the fruit of righteousness. It was just as Jesus warned would happen.

Look at this from Paul's point of view. Have you ever had a friend desert you? I have. How did it feel? It hurt, a lot. Did you have a hard time getting over it? Just think how Paul must have felt. One of the men he thought he could trust, a fellow Christian, just left at a time when Paul especially needed him. I imagine this hurt Paul worse than the shipwrecks and the beatings.

Then it dawned on me who else was hurt by the desertion of Demas – Christ. For truly Demas didn't only forsake Paul; he left his Savior. He returned to the old life, to the world. Demas stands out as a sharp contrast to Paul, who was faithful to the end.

What Lessons Do We Learn From Demas?

1. We must not let anything entice us away from God.

The fear of persecution and death coupled with the lure of the world may have been enough to pull Demas away from his faith. However, for a Christian, the thought of displeasing God and losing our souls for eternity should be our greatest fear. We are soldiers in a battle, and we must choose whether we will wear the uniform of Satan or the robes of righteousness. There is no middle ground. If we throw our lot in with God, we must not let anything pull us away from Him.

No one can serve two masters; for either he will hate the one and love the other, or else he will be loyal to the one and despise the other. You cannot serve God and mammon. (Matthew 6:24)

Do not love the world or the things in the world. If anyone loves the world, the love of the Father is not in him. For all that is in the world – the lust of the flesh, the lust of the eyes, and the pride of life – is not of the Father but is of the world. And the world is passing away, and the lust of it; but he who does the will of God abides forever. (1 John 2:15-17)

2. We must continue in our faith to the end.

Perhaps Paul was thinking of the departure of Demas when he wrote this familiar passage:

> I have fought the good fight, I have finished the race, I have kept the faith. Finally, there is laid up for me the crown of righteousness, which the LORD, the righteous Judge, will give to me on that Day, and not to me only but also to all who have loved His appearing. (2 Timothy 4:7-8)

Paul continued in his journey of faith, overcoming each obstacle that was in his path. He fought the good fight, finished the race and kept the faith. What a contrast to Demas who simply deserted his post!

We must "keep on keeping on." Think how enthusiastic we are when we start a new project. At first we are all gung-ho and excited, ready to do whatever it takes. But after a while it becomes routine, and we can become complacent. The excitement and that first rush of enthusiasm wear off. We struggle to keep our same level of commitment. This pattern holds true whether you are talking about a new job, a marriage, a fundraiser, a hobby or even faith. When your faith is new, you are eager and ready to face temptations, to study the Bible and to work for the Lord. But after a time, what happens? Your enthusiasm wanes; you get tired. Maybe you lose sight of the goal; you begin to remember your old life. Perhaps the hardest lesson we need to learn from Demas is to persist in the race, to continue throughout our entire lives to serve the Lord.

> And you, who once were alienated and enemies in your mind by wicked works, yet now He has reconciled in the body of His flesh through death, to present you holy, and blameless, and above reproach in His sight – if indeed you continue in the faith, grounded and steadfast, and are not moved away from the hope of the gospel which you heard, which was preached to every creature under heaven, of which I, Paul, became a minister. (Colossians 1:21-23)

3. We must remain faithful even if others depart from the faith.

Paul, even though he was a leader in the early church, could have been influenced by the departure of Demas. "Maybe Demas is right. Here I am stuck in this lonely prison, probably going to be put to death, and I didn't do anything wrong! How could God let this happen? Maybe I should go the way of Demas." Instead, Paul stayed faithful even when others around him did not. Paul had to deal with the lack of faith in others. In 2 Timothy 1:15, Paul informed us that Phygellus and Hermogenes also turned away from him. He could have felt like a failure; he could have become convinced that he was not accomplishing anything for the Lord. After all, people he had tried to teach were leaving the faith! But even after watching his fellow workers depart, Paul stayed faithful. We must not let the actions of others influence us to leave God; we must continue doing what we know to be right no matter what others around us do.

Let's Think About This

1. What pulls us away from God and back into the world? How do we overcome those things?

2. What are the biggest drawbacks you face as you strive to stay faithful?

3. Is it easy to stay faithful when those around you are abandoning their faith? Name some ways to help yourself and those around you stay true to God.

4. Our service to God may change as we grow older. Name specific ways senior saints can continue to serve God when their physical bodies slow down.

ONESIMUS:

From Slave to Brother

Philemon 1-25

We all know about slavery in this country preceding and during the time of the Civil War. Although we do not hear much about it, slavery is still rampant in the world today. Modern-day slaves can be found laboring as servants or concubines in Sudan, as child "carpet slaves" in India, or as cane-cutters in Pakistan, to name but a few instances.[1] According to the organization Anti-Slavery International, currently over 21 million men, women and children are in some form of slavery.[2] UNICEF estimates that 200,000 children are sold into slavery each year, some as young as 5 years old who were taken from their families. Sometimes slave runners will convince parents to let them take their children with promises of a good education and a better future only to force the children into a life of slavery. Many of these children are from countries in Africa and are sold into wealthier, neighboring countries such as Nigeria. In the U.S., cases of human trafficking have been reported in all 50 states.[3]

Can you imagine selling a person as you would a piece of furniture? It's impossible for us to picture such a thing. Slavery is nothing new; it has been common since ancient times. "Slavery was universal" in New Testament times. "Aristotle, one of the most enlightened of the Greeks, held that the Creator had made the majority of the human race for slavery. Even the Mosaic Law permitted [slavery], but with [certain regulations], which made Jewish slavery [by] far the mildest in the world. Under the Roman law, the slave was not considered a man, but a [possession] without any civil rights [whatsoever]"; the slave was "completely at the mercy of his master. The master could sell him, give him away, torture him, crucify him, put him to death, even feed him to his fish, and there was no law to [prevent it]."[4]

Under these conditions, many slaves through the years longed for their freedom. One slave not only desired to be free but tried to make it happen on his own terms. This lesson about the slave Onesimus is really a "twofer," two for the price of one. We cannot study the slave Onesimus without also studying his master, Philemon. The first part of their story we have to infer from what we are told.

Philemon was a good man who lived in the city of Colossae, which was close to Ephesus. Philemon evidently was at least somewhat wealthy, for he owned slaves. Slaves could be purchased; people captured in war frequently became slaves. The poor who were unable to pay their debts could offer themselves or their children as slaves. A thief who could not repay what he had stolen could also become a slave. Children born of slave parents became "house-born slaves."[5]

Somewhere along the way Philemon converted to Christianity. We are not told when this was, but we do know that Paul had a part in it. Sometime later Philemon became a leader in the Colossian church, even hosting the church in his home (Philemon 2).

One of Philemon's slaves was named Onesimus. How Onesimus became a slave is not disclosed to us. What we do know is that he ran away from his master. He escaped from Philemon and left the city of Colossae. During the time Paul was under house arrest in Rome, Onesimus evidently made his way to that city, came in contact with Paul, and was converted. Rome was more than 1,000 miles west of Colossae; it would have been a journey of many weeks. We wonder how a runaway slave could have made that long, dangerous trip.

While Paul was imprisoned in Rome, he wrote the letter to the Colossian church, what we know as Colossians, sometime around A.D. 62. At the same time, he also wrote a shorter, more personal letter to Philemon. The letter was directed particularly to Philemon because he was mentioned first. Apphia is thought to have been Philemon's wife and Archippus may have been their son.[6] It is evident that Philemon opened his home for worship as the church met in his house (Philemon 1-2).

Paul expressed his thankfulness for Philemon and his love and faith; Paul knew him to be a faithful Christian. *Willmington's Bible Handbook* suggests that Paul was buttering up Philemon by complimenting him so he would be agreeable to the coming request,[7] but perhaps he was just being gracious by beginning the letter with words of thanksgiving and praise to God. After the salutations came the real purpose of the letter.

Paul wrote that he had something he wanted Philemon to do, but he was not telling him outright to do it; he was just asking Philemon. However, Paul mentioned that he was an old man and in prison for Christ. Do we see a little arm-twisting persuasion here? Age demanded great respect at this time; thus, Paul mentioned being an old man. And he was in prison for preaching the gospel. He could have used his authority in the church to give a command to Philemon, but he didn't. After reminding Philemon of who was making the request, Paul mentioned the real reason for his letter – the slave Onesimus.

Paul referred to Onesimus as "my son" (Philemon 10), meaning his son in the faith. The name Onesimus means "profitable" or "useful."[8] Paul used a play on words in verse 11 when he said Onesimus "who once was unprofitable to you, but now is profitable to you and to me."

Paul would have liked for Onesimus to stay in Rome with him to offer help during Paul's imprisonment; however, Paul did the better thing by sending Onesimus home to Philemon. In his letter to the Christians in Colossae, we learn that Onesimus delivered this letter to his master Philemon himself.

> *Tychicus, a beloved brother, faithful minister, and fellow servant in the LORD, will tell you all the news about me. I am sending him to you for this very purpose, that he may know your circumstances and comfort your hearts, with Onesimus, a faithful and beloved brother, who is one of you. They will make known to you all things which are happening here. (Colossians 4:7-9)*

When a runaway slave was caught, he could be tortured or executed, but Paul sent Onesimus straight back to Philemon (Philemon 12-14). How difficult do you suppose it was for Onesimus to show up at Philemon's door? Was he trembling as he approached his former home?

These verses remind me of the saying attributed to Kahlil Gibran: "If you love somebody, let them go, for if they return, they were always yours. If they don't, they never were." Onesimus returned, not knowing how he would be received.

If Philemon accepted Onesimus back, the connection between them would be changed from master and slave, employer and employee, to brothers in the Lord (Philemon 15-16). How much better for both Philemon and Onesimus to be united in Christ! What a difference this would make in their relationship!

Paul encouraged Philemon not only to take Onesimus back but to welcome him the same as he would Paul himself. Paul promised that if Philemon had lost any money on account of Onesimus' absence, Paul would repay him (Philemon 17-18). It was as if Paul gave his personal IOU and said, "Just put it on my tab." Some Bible scholars believe that Onesimus stole money or property from Philemon when he ran away, but we do not know that for a fact. Paul may have been referring to the loss of labor during the absence of Onesimus. Whatever the loss, Paul pledged to pay the debt. Then, as an "and by the way," Paul added that he would not mention what Philemon owed him, which was "even your own self" (v. 19).

Paul had full confidence that Philemon would respond positively to his request. Because of the love Paul had for Philemon as well as his knowledge of Philemon's faithfulness to the Lord, Paul had every confidence that Philemon would receive Onesimus back into his household and treat him as a brother in Christ. Paul's comment – "knowing that you will do even more than I say" (Philemon 21) – may have been a hint even to grant Onesimus his freedom. It certainly puts a little added pressure on Philemon to do the right thing.

Paul closed this very personal letter with the hope to leave prison soon and go to Colossae. We do not know whether he ever did. Nor do the Scriptures tell us the end of Onesimus' story, but we would hope that at the very least Philemon forgave him and welcomed him back. Legend says Onesimus later became a leader in the early church.

What Lessons Do We Learn From Onesimus?

1. Forgiveness and reconciliation are possible if we love as Christ loved.

It is always tempting to run away from conflicts with other people, but that does not solve any problems. Nor does it help matters to respond to disagreements in an unchristian manner. The better way is reconciliation based on love. I heard a woman once say about a problem, "We can do this if we speak in love." That's what Paul was saying. Based on the love you have for others and the love we share in Christ, this can be worked out, and Onesimus can be accepted back as a brother.

2. Becoming a Christian does not negate the consequences of our past actions.

Onesimus could not say, "I am a Christian now and will live my life for God, but the past is over and done with." He had to make things right with Philemon. When we become Christians, our sins are forgiven, but we still have to face the consequences of our past actions. If an inmate in jail for a crime is converted to Christ, her jail sentence is not automatically revoked. She still must serve the remainder of her time in jail. If an alcoholic gives her life to Jesus in obedience to the gospel, she is still an alcoholic, but now she has God as her Father to help her fight her addiction. If we have hurt others by our actions or words, the damage may not be reversible. With God's help, we must deal with our past in a loving and Christlike way.

3. All men and women, whatever their circumstances, should display love and respect for one another.

Many of the early Christian congregations were made up of a large number of slaves and some slave owners. They had to learn that, in Christ, all men are equal.

There is neither Jew nor Greek, there is neither slave nor free, there is neither male nor female; for you are all one in Christ Jesus. (Galatians 3:28)

All people deserve our love and respect because each one is important to God. God created and loves each person. He loves the middle-class mother in the U.S. just the same as the poverty-stricken child in Africa; He loves the leaders and kings of the world as well as the migrant workers in the fields. God has provided the way of salvation for all people, making no distinction among them.

4. We are thankful for our Mediator, Jesus Christ.

Martin Luther is quoted as saying, "Even as Christ did for us with God the Father, thus also does Paul for Onesimus with Philemon."[9] Paul acted as a mediator between Philemon and Onesimus, bringing them back together in a new relationship. Think how terribly dangerous it would have been for Onesimus to approach Philemon without that letter from Paul. Our Mediator is Jesus Christ. He has become our Mediator with God, paving the way for forgiveness and a reunion with the Father, even at the cost of His own life. We are blessed to know the love of a Mediator, Savior and Friend.

*And for this reason He is the Mediator of the new covenant,
by means of death, for the redemption of the transgressions
under the first covenant, that those who are called may receive
the promise of the eternal inheritance. (Hebrews 9:15)*

Let's Think About This

1. Why did Paul send Onesimus back to Philemon? How does Ephesians 6:5-9 apply in this situation?

2. Why did Paul choose not to command Philemon to take Onesimus back?

3. Why didn't Paul abolish slavery altogether?

4. How do you handle disagreements with employers or co-workers?

5. How do you handle disagreements with Christian brothers or sisters? How should those differences be resolved?

6. What do we do about past sins that cannot be made right?

Endnotes

Chapter 1

1. "Jericho." *Nelson's Illustrated Bible Dictionary*, PC Study Bible V5. Ed. Herbert Lockyer. (Biblesoft, Inc., 1988-2013). Computer software.

2. Keener, Craig S. *The IVP Bible Background Commentary: New Testament*. (Downers Grove: InterVarsity Press, 1993). 240.

3. Wiersbe, Warren W. "The Savior Who Seeks the Lost (Luke 19:1-10)." *The Bible Exposition Commentary: New Testament*, PC Study Bible V5. (Biblesoft, Inc., 1988–2013). Computer software.

4. "Luke 19:5." *The Greek Hebrew Dictionary*, PC Study Bible V5. (Biblesoft, Inc., 1988-2013). Computer software.

5. "Luke 19:6." *The Greek-Hebrew Dictionary*.

6. Jamieson, Robert, A.R. Fausset and David Brown. "Luke 19:8." *Jamieson, Fausset, and Brown Commentary*, PC Study Bible V5. (Biblesoft, Inc., 1988–2013). Computer software.

7. Willmington, Harold L. "Zacchaeus." *Willmington's Bible Handbook*, PC Study Bible V5. (Biblesoft, Inc., 1988–2013). Computer software.

8. Wiersbe. "The Savior Who Seeks the Lost (Luke 19:1-10)."

Chapter 2

1. Heidebrecht, Paul and Ted Scheuermann. "Nathanael." *Men Like Us*. (Wheaton: Harold Shaw Publishers, 1993). 67.

2. Barnes, Albert. "John 1:48." *Barnes' Notes*, PC Study Bible V5. (Biblesoft, Inc., 1988–2013). Computer software.

Chapter 3

1. Carson, D.A. "The Gospel According to John." *The Pillar New Testament Commentary*. (Grand Rapids: Eerdmans Publishing Company, 1991). 186.

2. Barnes, Albert. "John 3:5." *Barnes' Notes*, PC Study Bible V5. (Biblesoft, Inc., 1988–2013). Computer software.

3. Wiersbe, Warren W. "Christ Buried (19:31-42)." *The Bible Exposition Commentary: New Testament*, PC Study Bible V5. (Biblesoft, Inc., 1988-2013). Computer software.

4. Henry, Matthew. "John 19:38-42." *Matthew Henry's Commentary on the Whole Bible*, PC Study Bible V5. (Biblesoft, Inc., 1988–2013). Computer software.

5. "Nicodemus." *Nelson's Illustrated Bible Dictionary*, PC Study Bible V5. Ed. Herbert Lockyer. (Biblesoft, Inc., 1988–2013). Computer software.

Chapter 4

1. Keener, Craig S. *The IVP Bible Background Commentary: New Testament*. (Downers Grove: InterVarsity Press, 1993). 288.

2. Henry, Matthew. "John 9:1-7." *Matthew Henry's Commentary on the Whole Bible*, PC Study Bible V5. (Biblesoft, Inc., 1988–2013). Computer software.

3. "The Miracle of Sight." *Sermoncentral.com*. Outreach Inc. April 2011. Web. 25 July 2016.

4. Keener. 288.

5. Henry. "John 9:1-7."

Chapter 5

1. Barnes, Albert. "John 11:16." *Barnes' Notes*, PC Study Bible V5. (Biblesoft, Inc., 1988–2013). Computer software.

2. Keener, Craig S. *The IVP Bible Background Commentary: New Testament*. (Downers Grove: InterVarsity Press, 1993). 317.

3. Swindoll, Charles R. *Growing Deep in the Christian Life*. (Portland: Multnomah Press, 1986). 169.

Chapter 6

1. "Playing Darts." *Bible.org*. Bible.org. 02 Feb. 2009. Web. 25 July 2016.

2. "William Arthur Ward." *Thinkexist.com*. ThinkExist. Web. 1 Aug. 2016.

3. Keener, Craig S. *The IVP Bible Background Commentary: New Testament*. (Downers Grove: InterVarsity Press, 1993). 334.

4. Schnabel, Eckhard J. "Acts." *Zondervan Exegetical Commentary on the New Testament*. (Grand Rapids: Zondervan, 2012). 273.

Chapter 7

1. Robertson, A.T. "Ananias and Sapphira or the First Ananias Club." *Some Minor Characters in the New Testament*. (Grand Rapids: Baker, 1928). 169-70.

2. "Burial." *Nelson's Illustrated Bible Dictionary*, PC Study Bible V5. Ed. Herbert Lockyer. (Biblesoft, Inc., 1988-2013). Computer software.

3. *Zondervan King James Version Commentary New Testament*. Ed. Edward E. Hindson and Daniel R. Mitchell. (Grand Rapids: Zondervan, 2010). 342.

4. Eichman, Nancy. *Seasoning Your Words*. 2nd ed. (Nashville: Gospel Advocate Publishing Co., 2015). 46.

5. Lockyer, Herbert. "Ananias." *All the Men of the Bible*. (Grand Rapids: Zondervan, 1958). 48-49.

6. Cillizza, Chris and Paul Kane. "John Ensign to Retire in 2012." *The Washington Post*. 7 Mar. 2011. Web. 1 Aug. 2016.

Chapter 8

1. "Hospitality." *Nelson's Illustrated Bible Dictionary*, PC Study Bible V5. Ed. Herbert Lockyer. (Biblesoft, Inc., 1988-2013). Computer software.

2. Exum, Jack. *Questions You Have Asked About Soul Winning*. (Fort Worth: Star Bible Publications, 1963). 19.

Chapter 9

1. Whyte, Alexander. "Eutychus." *Whyte's Dictionary of Bible Characters*. *StudyLight.org*. Web. 1 Aug. 2016.

2. "Eutychus." *Encyclopedia of the Bible*. *Bible Gateway*. The Zondervan Corporation. Web. 13 Sept. 2015.

3. Lockyer, Herbert. "Eutychus." *All the Men of the Bible*. (Grand Rapids: Zondervan, 1958). 115.

4. Clarke, Adam. "Acts 20:7." *Adam Clarke's Commentary*, PC Study Bible V5. (Biblesoft, Inc.,1988–2013). Computer software.

5. Henry, Matthew. "Acts 20:7-12." *Matthew Henry's Commentary on the Whole Bible*, PC Study Bible V5. (Biblesoft, Inc., 1988–2013). Computer software.

6. Wiersbe, Warren W. "A Farewell Service (Acts 20:6-12)," *The Bible Exposition Commentary: New Testament*, PC Study Bible V5. (Biblesoft, Inc., 1988–2013). Computer software.

7. Heidebrecht, Paul and Ted Scheuermann. "Eutychus." *Men Like Us*. (Wheaton: Harold Shaw, 1993). 56.

8. Swindoll, Charles R. "Sleeping in Church." *Come Before Winter*. (Portland: Multnomah Press, 1985). 185-86.

9. List paraphrased from Swindoll's *Come Before Winter*.

Chapter 10

1. Smith, William. "Philip." *Smith's Bible Dictionary*. Bible Study Tools. Salem Communications. 2014. Web. 1 Aug. 2016.

2. "Philip." *Encyclopedia of the Bible*. *Bible Gateway*. The Zondervan Corporation. Web. 13 Sept. 2015.

3. Willmington, Harold L. "The Son of Man Ministers to Humankind (4:14-9:50)." *Willmington's Bible Handbook*, PC Study Bible V5. (Biblesoft, Inc., 1988–2013). Computer software.

4. Lockyer, Herbert. "Philip." *All the Men of the Bible*. (Grand Rapids: Zondervan, 1958). 277.

5. "Philip (2)." *International Standard Bible Encyclopedia*. *Bible Study Tools*. Salem Communications. 2014. Web. 1 Aug. 2016.

Chapter 11

1. Jamieson, Robert, A.R. Fausset and David Brown. "Acts 6:1." *Jamieson, Fausset, and Brown Commentary*, PC Study Bible V5. (Biblesoft, Inc., 1988–2013). Computer software.

2. Wiersbe, Warren W. "Philip the Evangelist (8:1-25)." *The Bible Exposition Commentary: New Testament*, PC Study Bible V5, (Biblesoft, Inc., 1988–2013). Computer software.

3. Wiersbe. "A Concerned Seeker – an Ethiopian (Acts 8:26-40)."

4. Clarke, Adam. "Acts 8:27." *Adam Clarke's Commentary*, PC Study Bible V5. (Biblesoft, Inc.,1988–2013). Computer software.

5. Schnabel, Eckhard J. "Acts." *Zondervan Exegetical Commentary on the New Testament*. (Grand Rapids: Zondervan, 2012). 426.

Chapter 12

1. "Scroll." *Nelson's Illustrated Bible Dictionary*, PC Study Bible V5. Ed. Herbert Lockyer. (Biblesoft, Inc., 1988-2013). Computer software.

2. Lockyer, Herbert. "Demas." *All the Men of the Bible*. (Grand Rapids: Zondervan, 1958). 92.

3. Henry, Matthew. "2 Timothy 4:9-15." *Matthew Henry's Commentary on the Whole Bible*, PC Study Bible V5. (Biblesoft, Inc., 1988–2013).

Chapter 13

1. Goldberg, Eleanor. "The Subhuman Conditions That Slaves and Child Laborers Face in India Are Worse Than You Imagined (HOW TO HELP)." *The Huffington Post*. 13 March 2014. Web. 2 Aug. 2016.

2. "What Is Modern Slavery?" *Anti-Slavery*. Anti-Slavery International. Web. 26 July 2016.

3. "Child Trafficking." *UNICEF United States Fund*. U.S. Fund for UNICEF. Web. 2 Aug. 2016.

4. Johnson, B.W. *The People's New Testament With Explanatory Notes*. (Nashville: Gospel Advocate Company). 292.

5. "Slave, Slavery." *Nelson's Illustrated Bible Dictionary*, PC Study Bible V5. Ed. Herbert Lockyer. (Biblesoft, Inc., 1988–2013). Computer software.

6. Clarke, Adam. "Philemon 1-2." *Adam Clarke's Commentary*, PC Study Bible V5. (Biblesoft, Inc.,1988–2013). Computer software.

7. Willmington, Harold L. "Commending Philemon (1:1-7)." *Willmington's Bible Handbook*, PC Study Bible V5. (Biblesoft, Inc., 1988-2013). Computer software.

8. Hitchcock, Roswell Dwight. "Onesimus." *Hitchcock's Bible Names Dictionary*, PC Study Bible V5. (Biblesoft, Inc., 1988–2013). Computer software.

9. "Philemon 1." *Guzik Bible Commentary*. *Bible Hub*. Bible Hub. Web. 2 Aug. 2016.

CPSIA information can be obtained
at www.ICGtesting.com
Printed in the USA
LVOW03s0040130617
537896LV00001B/2/P